GARRY MICHAEL

The Reaper

Copyright © 2023 by Garry Michael

All rights reserved. No part of this publication may be reproduced, stored or transmitted in any form or by any means, electronic, mechanical, photocopying, recording, scanning, or otherwise without written permission from the publisher. It is illegal to copy this book, post it to a website, or distribute it by any other means without permission.

This novel is entirely a work of fiction. The names, characters and incidents portrayed in it are the work of the author's imagination. Any resemblance to actual persons, living or dead, events or localities is entirely coincidental.

Designations used by companies to distinguish their products are often claimed as trademarks. All brand names and product names used in this book and on its cover are trade names, service marks, trademarks and registered trademarks of their respective owners. The publishers and the book are not associated with any product or vendor mentioned in this book. None of the companies referenced within the book have endorsed the book.

First edition

Editing by Ebony Stokes
Editing by Carlie Slattery
Cover art by Roopali Designs
Translation by Amarilys S.M.

This book was professionally typeset on Reedsy.
Find out more at reedsy.com

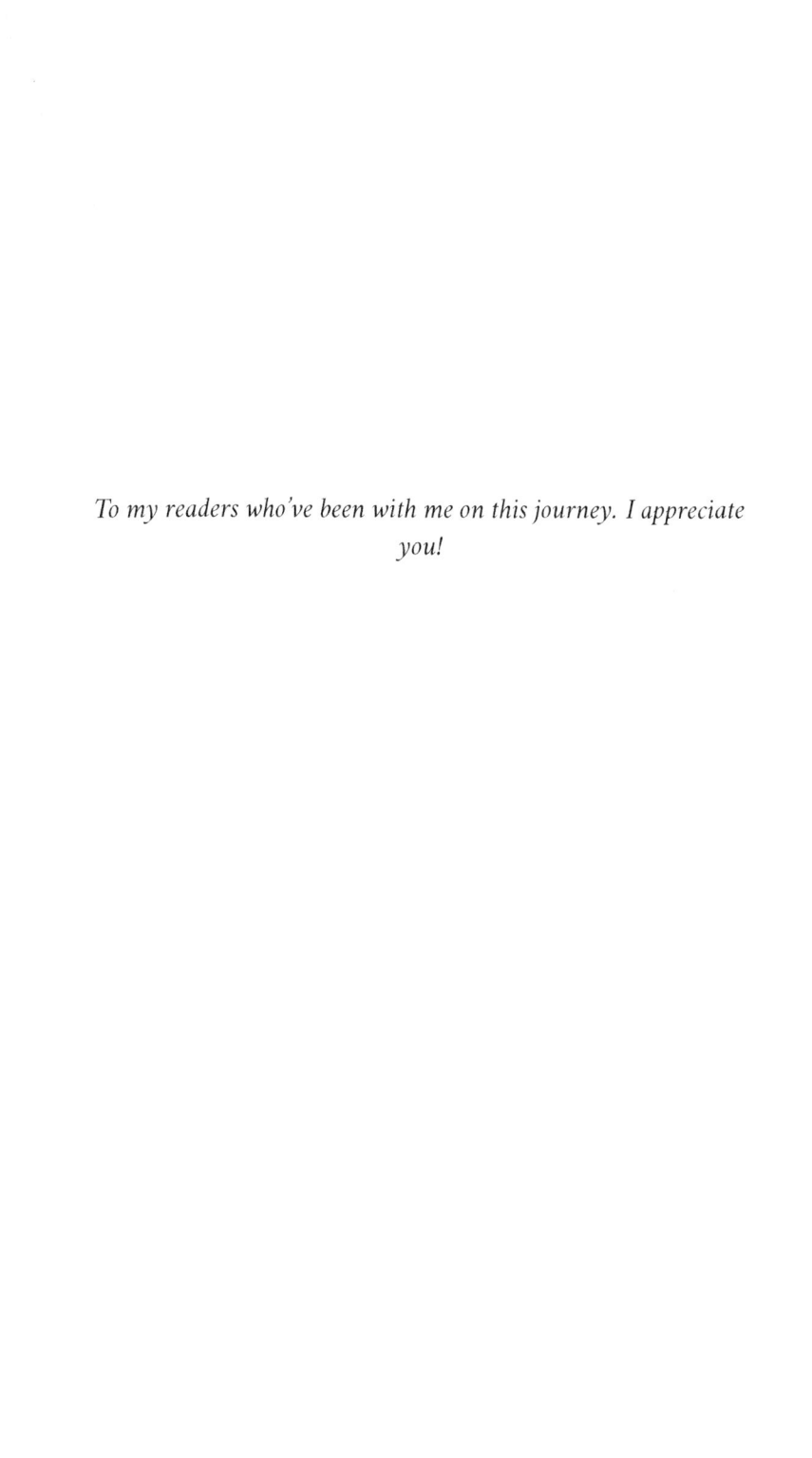

To my readers who've been with me on this journey. I appreciate you!

Sometimes, justice isn't obvious.

    Archer, The Reaper

Contents

Acknowledgement	iii
Trigger Warning	v
One: The Reaper	1
Two: The Reaper	6
Three: The Priest	11
Four: The Reaper	18
Five: The Priest	25
Six: The Reaper	35
Seven: The Priest	46
Eight: The Reaper	53
Nine: The Priest	61
Ten: The Reaper	68
Eleven: The Priest	75
Twelve: The Reaper	83
Thirteen: The Priest	90
Fourteen: The Reaper	96
Fifteen: The Priest	104
Sixteen: The Reaper	116
Seventeen: The Priest	124
Eighteen: The Reaper	130
Nineteen: The Priest	144
Twenty: The Reaper	152
Twenty-One: The Priest	161
Twenty-Two: The Reaper	167

Twenty-Three: The Priest	175
Twenty-Four: The Reaper	183
Twenty-Five: The Priest	193
Twenty-Six: The Reaper	201
Twenty-Seven: The Priest	208
Twenty-Eight: The Reaper	213
Twenty-Nine: The Priest	222
Thirty: The Reaper	231
Thirty-One: The Priest	239
Thirty-Two: The Reaper	246
Thirty-Three: The Priest	256
Thirty-Four: The Reaper	262
Thirty-Five: The Priest	273
About the Author	279
Also by Garry Michael	280

Acknowledgement

This Journey has been the most exciting and nerve-wracking experience of my life. I've met great people along the way and I will be forever thankful for the wisdom, love and support.

To Mr. Z- I love you to the moon and back.

To my Mom and Dad who have encouraged me to ALWAYS be true to myself. I never had to come out because you knew all along and never made me feel less than amazing.

To my brothers and sisters. This is for you.

To my partner in crime, Jeris Jean- Thanks for being an amazing friend and cheerleader.

To Michaela Cole- Thank you for sharing your knowledge and for always being an extra set of eyes with everything I do.

E.B. Slayer & Carlie- Thank you, for being a great advisor.

To all the amazing Independent Authors. I apologize in advance if I miss you. Please know that I appreciate all of you.- Tempest Phan, C.M. Danks, Swati M.H, Sue Watts, Matthew Dante, Devin Sloane, S.M Lanyon, Miss Mock, Janice Jarrell, Jenni Barra, Lizzie Stanley, Selena Moore, Zee Shine Storm, Barbara Kellyn, N. Dune, Nola Marie, P.K Morrison. Sionna Trenz, Monica Arya, Aurora Page, Ish, Ruby Ana, Charm White, Anna Fury, Elle Bor, Ducky Mack, Ashlyn Drewek, Sana Khari, Azalea Hudson, Samantha Thomas, Stacy Kristen, Melonay Ann, Jen Samson, Lola Malone, Dianna Roman, Courtney Dixon, and Robert Karl.

To all the book bloggers and fanatics who help me spread the word about my books. Dawn, Tina, Jamie, April, Brittany, Lyndsay, Stefka, Gena, the Emmas, Amy V., Renate, Jenny, Amarilys, Anna, Marla, Michelle, Anita, Jenny, Melissa, Nedra, Jerrica, Taima, Tammy, Katherine, Anita, Kel, Andrea, Ayana, Myri, Heidi, Emily, Niki, Missy, Anja, and all the bookstagrammers.

To my ARC readers- you are all AMAZING

Thank you, Amarilys for translating (Spanish) for me. I appreciate your help!

To Roopali, thank you for the great cover designs and for always accommodating my last minute requests.

To Sam and Dar who think I can do no wrong. I love you both.

Elly - Thank you for answering all my cop related questions.

Elly and Reenie, two of my fave people. Thanks for adding joy to our lives.

Last but not the least, the readers. We are nothing without you. THANK YOU FROM THE BOTTOM OF MY HEART.

Trigger Warning

The Reaper contains elements of dark romance, gruesome and violent scenes including murder, and religious sexual explorations. If you've read any of my previously published works, you might find this book on the darker side of the spectrum.

One: The Reaper

Havana

An extraordinary life: the currency upon which men in the shadows were built. Ironic, considering how hard we tried to live, breathe, and act behind obscurity. What I wouldn't give to be an ordinary man, living an unremarkable life.

The bell tower from the nearby church rang, a relic reminding those who could hear it of the time—high noon. Like most of Latin America, Cuba was steeped in Catholic traditions, pressures that guilted the living from those who'd turned to dust. I would know. I wasn't proud to admit it, but I succumbed to the pressure every now and then. Who was I kidding? It was a compulsion. Call it insurance just in case *they* were right.

I looked up at the blue Havana sky between the rows of preserved Spanish colonial-style buildings painted bright colors, stamping them with Caribbean identity. The blistering heat was a reprieve from the bone-chilling cold of Boston's brutal winter. There was no getting used to that weather, but if there was one great byproduct of New England's winter, it was the prolonged darkness where I found my solace.

Sweat trickled down my forehead into the slanted crease above my left eye. A scar. A daily reminder of what could happen if I let my guard down. After quenching my thirst with a gulp of lemonade sweetened with fresh sugarcane juice, I leaned back in the iron chair, soaking every bit of sun I could take until my skin punished me with a burn.

Far away, a speeding car revved, making me uneasy. Its tires kissed the road with haste and purpose. It sounded heavy, possibly an SUV. It could be nothing, but I kept my ears and eyes on high alert.

Patrons were unfazed as they sipped their Cuban espresso out in the open-air café along the street lined with pastel-colored vintage American cars from the sixties—like crayons on the cobblestone ground.

"¡Hola, hermana!" a statuesque woman dressed to the nines exclaimed, greeting an equally striking woman. They shared similar almond-shaped light brown eyes, golden skin, and shiny black hair. Their resemblance was uncanny.

A couple more joined them, exchanging boomerangs of cheek kisses planted on both sides of their made-up faces. They took their seats, straightening their floral sundresses to keep them wrinkle-free, seemingly unaware of the potential threat looming.

One of the ladies glanced my way, appraising me from head to toe. Interest was written all over her gaze. Her matte red lips parted in a smile. She leaned closer to the table and whispered something, causing everyone to giggle. *"He's so sexy, no?"* I didn't hear the words that came out of her mouth, but I was an expert at reading lips.

I adjusted my position, uncrossing my legs before placing my right hand on my thigh, inches away from the gun tucked into my white linen pants. The first three buttons of the matching shirt were free. I cocked my head and fixed my sunglasses, trying to discern which direction the car was going—approaching or receding? It was a habit formed out of necessity.

A group of middle-aged men wearing tan straw hats passed by on the sidewalk. Their body language appeared docile and non-threatening, but my sight traveled to their waists searching for signs of any weapons and assessing levels of danger. I could never be too sure in my line of work. I'd seen it all, and no one would ever surprise me again.

The revving grew louder, nearer.

My whole body tensed, bracing for what was coming. Revving no longer suggested a speeding car impatiently navigating streets, or youngsters being youngsters. As a trained assassin, it held a different significance. These days, revving was followed by shots and, on rare occasions, explosions. Revving could mean a *hit*. It could mean a suicide bomber plowing through a crowd of people indiscriminate of their victims.

It could mean death.

A small child walking behind his mother—who was involved in a one-way conversation on the phone—stopped and stared at my face. You couldn't miss the fascination in his innocent brown eyes. Perhaps he was playing a game of 'One of These Things is Not Like the Others' among the locals and me. My blond hair stood out like a sore thumb among the sea of brunettes. I should've worn a hat.

The speeding car was closing in.

"*¡Puta madrè!*" someone yelled from a distance through screeching brake pads. Horns blasted. Disrupted city pigeons took flight.

The kid was still staring, his mother was twenty feet away.

He's gotta go. Having a child as collateral damage if this day went south wasn't how I wanted to spend my afternoon. I removed my sunglasses, exposing my scarred eye, and snarled at him.

His mouth opened wide. "Mama!" he cried, running away in the direction of his mother, who extended her hand to grab his. *Good.*

A black SUV came into view. All its windows were tinted opaque. The back-seat window slid open, revealing the nose of a rifle.

Terror amassed in me. Not for myself, but for everyone around me. *"¡Quédate abajo!"* I yelled, urging everyone to duck. These men were undeniably gunning for me.

It was havoc. Porcelains shattered on the ground, screams and clatters filled the air. People were pulling, pushing, and tripping on their dash to the exit, others hid under the tables and prayed. A succession of shots was fired and heat scored my left arm before I managed to get behind a concrete half-wall. Bullets pierced through windows and glass vases, flowers were everywhere—what was left of them anyway. More shots followed. Debris from the concrete wall floated, causing some patrons to cough.

I peeked around the side. I withdrew my gun and aimed it at the speeding car as it passed, memorizing the set of numbers on its plate: *Rep. Cuba. 122–500 Havana.* I fired, managing to hit the back of the car, shattering its rear window. "Shit! Shit! Shit!"

I looked back at the café; all horror-struck eyes were on me. No one appeared to be hurt, thankfully.

Blood had dyed my sleeve red as it seeped through the white linen.

I patted the source of the blood. A sharp pain radiated from my deltoid when my fingers brushed the shallow wound. The bullet had passed through and was probably lodged in the wall behind me.

Sirens wailed from two different directions, becoming louder as they neared.

"Fuck!" I got up and sprinted to the narrow alley, bumping into people along the way. The last thing I needed was for the local authority to wonder who I was, or worse, detain me for more questioning. For once in my life, I wasn't in the know—not that I would tell them anything anyway.

One thing I knew for certain: this wasn't a random shooting. Yet no one knew where I was. *So who the fuck was after me?*

Two: The Reaper

Boston

I chose to live my life in the shadows, and one day, it would get me killed. That realization had stuck with me from the moment I picked up a gun. I was the best in the business, and the more times I pulled the trigger, the closer I came to my inevitable end.

It had been three months since the incident in Havana, and it had taken the same amount of time to hunt the men responsible for the strike against me. I would've traced them sooner had I not kept a low profile for a month to plan my course of action.

"Lie low for now and we'll figure this out," El Jefe, the brains of our operations, had said when I made it to his office, fuming. It was the first place I visited when my feet touched the ground from Cuba three months ago after the attack. It'd been a close call, and if it wasn't for my vigilance, I would've been one of the nameless men from The Firm's roster who met their peril year after year. He was as stunned as I was about the attack, but that didn't stop me from grilling him.

"That was not fucking random!" I yelled, slamming my hands on his oak desk. A silver tray containing glasses and a decanter rattled from the force.

The door opened and one of the men assigned to protect El Jefe rushed in, hand resting on his holster. His head mimicked that of a tennis umpire, eyes bouncing between El Jefe and me, but I didn't give a fuck. Truth be told, I didn't have a lot of fucks to give at all, and I'd be damned if I gave one then. My fucks were reserved for special occasions and that wasn't it.

El Jefe raised his hand, stopping him. "We're okay," he said, nodding toward the door. "The Reaper just got a little ..." He trailed off, pressing his index finger to his lips. "Excited." He leaned back in his black leather chair, his favorite drink in his other hand. "Whiskey?" he offered when his minion was out of sight. He poured the varnish-colored liquid into another glass, sliding it toward the edge of his desk.

That served to piss me off. I didn't come here for chit-chat. I needed answers. *Now.* "Tell me what you know and don't fucking lie to me," I said. My jaw was clenched so hard my teeth could shatter.

He looked me straight in the eye and said, "I ain't got no answer cuz I got nothin' to tell you, kid." He drew the glass snifter to his mouth, never breaking eye contact as he polished off its contents. A sigh escaped him, perhaps enjoying the burn of alcohol in his throat. "You sure they're after you?"

"One hundred percent," I said before gulping the drink he'd offered.

He was thoughtful for a while, rubbing his graying beard with his hand. What I wouldn't give to know what was on his mind. The Firm might not have shared everything with him, but he always knew more than he should. And right now, his poker face was impeccable. "That's not good," he said after a couple of minutes.

I studied his face, thinking about the first time I met him twelve years ago, on my nineteenth birthday. Days after I was sentenced to life for a crime I didn't commit. The day I lost faith in the system, the system that failed me when it was supposed to protect me. The day I buried the old me to become the man I was now.

El Jefe's gaze traveled to the scar on my face. "I'll get to the bottom of things," he assured me, and I believed him. He was one of the very few people I trusted. And in my world, trust was priceless. He'd never given me a reason to doubt him. In fact, El Jefe had treated me like a son, and I looked up to him like a father. A void men like us filled for each other because we wouldn't dare try to have a family. It was a liability. We were the harbingers of death and it snuffed out everyone in our lives.

"Figure it out fast—or I will," I said. "And I won't have mercy."

It wasn't a threat but a promise, and after months of waiting, I'd had enough.

***

I poured two fingers of vodka into a crystal glass before sliding the pair of leather gloves back onto my hands. After taking a big gulp and another drag of my cigarette, I moved back inside the old shipping container covered with a heavy-duty plastic tarp. I'd never been a smoker, but it had been a ritual before and after every kill. It was a habit I'd learned early on to take the edge off watching the light disappear from their eyes.

The two amateur hitmen's sloppy job had made it easy for me to track them down. Using a real name to book a rental car was a fucking rookie mistake.

"What do you want? Money?" one of the hitmen asked, mumbling his words through busted lips. He wiggled his body in a lame attempt to free himself from the metal chair he'd been chained to since the previous night. He leaned forward, squinting through his swollen purple eyelids, perhaps to make out who his captor was in the dark. Tears and snot dripped down his blood-covered face. "I have plenty. Whatever you need. Just spare me," he pleaded before glancing to his right where his lifeless confidant sat, adorned with a single bullet hole in his forehead.

That ridiculous statement made me laugh. It was a lie. He wouldn't be here, begging for his life, if he had *plenty* of money. The videos captured by CCTV where the failed ambush took place led me to this dynamic duo with a rap sheet longer than a line at an all-you-can-eat buffet.

"Oh god!" he wailed. Another squirm followed by a hop caused the chair to skid on the floor.

The grating sound pierced my eardrums, but I remained silent. My elbow rested on the armrest, a pistol in my hand aimed at his battered head. My finger curled over the trigger. Waiting for these men to croak was getting old, and patience had never been my strongest suit, especially after vetting Dumb and Dumber here only to find roadblock after roadblock. Whoever hired these two knew what they were doing, and that was making me uneasy.

Minutes passed, waiting for the fucker to break.

"They'll find you, motherfucker," he yelled when his cash offering failed.

I thought, until recently, that I no longer existed to the rest of the world. Twelve years ago, I died. Well, not literally, but I was a nobody. These two idiots shouldn't have known how to find me.

"And when they do, they will—"

A single bang echoed through the small room and I watched as his head fell back, blood splattering the wall and dripping onto the plastic-covered floor. I looked down at my smoking gun, my only friend, before wiping a drop of blood spray from my cheek with my glove.

This life would kill me, no doubt about it, but not today. I would find whoever was after me if it was the last thing I did.

Three: The Priest

In some ways, my arrival at the Cathedral of Holy Cross in Boston felt like a reset. An opportunity to be someone new; a second chance to redeem myself in the place I once called home. Poetic, but the path that led me back there was long and tumultuous—how being reborn should be. The distance between the high desert of Albuquerque and the seaside of Boston was nothing but a closed chapter of my life.

It was late in the evening when I arrived in front of what was to be my new home. Father Oller was waiting on the curb when I came out of the town car they'd arranged to pick me up. The moon was full, while the stars fought the city lights for attention. Father Oller didn't know it, but we'd met almost twenty years ago, when I was ten years old. A life of servitude had withered him. His blue eyes were dulled by the milky circles around his pupils. I was unsure if it was the moon casting a gray hue on his short hair that made it appear lighter than I remembered, but he'd definitely aged. "You must be Father Saint James," he greeted, leaning forward to look behind me. "The bishop's house to your left is unlocked," he instructed the driver carrying my two suitcases.

I shook both of his hands before handing him the letter from the Vatican about my new mission to replace the parish's longtime bishop. "It's nice to finally meet you," I said, examining his face. Either he was great at masking his disappointment or he wasn't bothered by my arrival and his impending relocation.

Father Oller rested his reading glasses on the bridge of his nose. He flipped the envelope open, his head moving side to side as he read the letter. "Let me show you around," he said moments later, handing the letter back to me. Still no expression. I marched behind him as he led me to my new residence. "This way," he instructed when he turned left. He needn't have bothered because I knew this place like the back of my hand. Still, I played along. "Everything you need is here. Jessica will be in tomorrow morning to help you get settled." He stood to the side of the open door, where my bags were parked on the stone steps.

Confused, I asked, "You're not coming in?" I didn't expect him to leave so soon. The bishop's residence could easily accommodate both of us.

Father Oller reached for my hand, placing the keys on my open palm. "No. My flight leaves tonight."

"Well, thank you, Father Oller," I said, shaking his hands. "I promise to take care of the parish."

"I'm sure you will, son."

***

A couple of days later, I glanced at my reflection before heading out of the bishop's house. *Just like any other mission,* I told myself.

THREE: THE PRIEST

My new home was separated from the church by a courtyard, with a garden outlined by boxwood. Red and yellow tulips were in bloom, while floral baskets bursting with different colors hung on every pillar of the cloister leading to the equally impressive cathedral made out of pale terracotta bricks.

The mosaic stained glass filtering the morning sun, and the smoke issuing from the incense sticks and candles on the altar, gave the church a heavenly glow. The ornate Hook and Hastings brass organ hadn't changed since I'd last seen it when I was a teenager. The memories of those years were preserved just like every nook and cranny of this place. I could still hear my uncle's voice whenever I closed my eyes: *"You have big shoes to fill."* We were a family of priests. Two of my uncles were priests, and my older brother was too.

I made my way to the altar, pulled a gold and jade rosary from the pocket of my black pants, and kneeled. Jesus on the cross looked down at me, and I wondered about the things he'd seen, the secrets he'd heard. Bowing my head with my joined hands, I prayed, adding weight to the savior's shoulders.

I had barely begun when the old, heavy wooden door creaked open, carrying babble through the nave of the church. With my eyes closed, I traced the tiny smooth body of Christ carved in the small cross in my hands. The chatter continued as my fingers glided through the first three beads, in sync with the words etched in my mind. I could tell where I was with my prayers just by feeling every groove of my chaplet.

The conversation among the new arrivals halted, replaced by the sound of footsteps and faint murmurs.

"Now might not be the best time," a soft, familiar female voice whispered.

"It won't take long," a deeper male voice said.

"We just want to introduce ourselves," a woman with a thick New England accent insisted.

"Fine," the first woman said to cover her sigh.

Their steady strides continued, becoming louder as they neared me. My concentration had been broken. My curiosity piqued, and I resorted to a shortened version of my prayer.

Someone cleared their throat when they reached the bottom of the high altar in the middle of the cathedral. "Um, Father?" the same familiar voice asked hesitantly. "Mr. and Mrs. Callahan would like to say hello."

"Is he the one who replaced Father Oller? He looks so young," the man whispered.

I lifted my head. "In the name of the Father, the Son, and the Holy Spirit. Amen," I said, signing the cross before rising.

Jessica, the parish assistant I'd met the day after I arrived two days ago, stood next to an older couple with big smiles on their faces. "I hope we're not interrupting." She walked toward me and extended her hand.

"Thank you, Jessica," I said, handing her my rosary. "And you're not interrupting. Your timing is perfect."

She smiled and pocketed the chain of beads before introducing me to our guests. "This is Mr. Spencer Callahan and his wife, Mrs. Marcella Callahan." Jessica stood next to me motioning to our guests. "They *sponsored* the remodeling of the west wing and the bishop's residence last year."

I didn't miss the way Jessica emphasized *sponsored*. Every parish had one or a hundred. "Oh, of course," I said, and closed the distance between myself and the Callahans. "I've heard a lot of great things about you." I offered my hand to Mrs. Callahan first. "It's nice to finally meet you."

Mrs. Callahan beamed. "Welcome to Boston, Father Saint

THREE: THE PRIEST

James," she said.

I switched my attention to Mr. Callahan, who was standing proudly. "On behalf of the parish, we'd like to thank both of you for your generosity." I shook his hand, giving them my most genuine smile.

"It's our pleasure," Mr. Callahan said. "We wanted to meet Father Oller's replacement as soon as we heard of his reassignment. His move was abrupt. I hope he's okay," he continued, rubbing Mrs. Callahan's back. He eyed me, his smile fading. His stare made my skin crawl.

"He is doing very well," I said. "Father Oller had always wanted to travel to Southeast Asia, so it was Godsent, truly."

"That's good to hear," Mrs. Callahan said. "So, to whom do we owe the pleasure of having you in Boston?" she asked, transferring her small leather purse to her other hand. "Is this your first parish? You seem too young to be leading this size of congregation. Is this temporary?"

"I think we should let Father rest. He's been meeting parishioners all morning and I'm sure he's tired," Jessica interrupted.

"It's okay, Jessica," I said. She was being kind, rescuing me from the barrage of questions Mr. and Mrs. Callahan were throwing at me, but I was used to it. *They mean no harm*, I told myself. They were just curious. I faced the couple, meeting their inquisitive gazes. "I led parishes in Albuquerque and San Luis Obispo prior."

The couple nodded, appearing unsatisfied. "But you sound like you're a local," Mrs. Callahan commented. They stared at my face, and then at Jessica, waiting for more information.

"Boston is home for me. I was born and raised here before heading west to study theology. And as far as age …" I paused and walked toward the front of the church.

Jessica and the Callahans followed.

"Although I'm only thirty years old, I can assure you that the church is in great hands," I said. The three of them kept pace with my stride. "I can't express how thankful I am for this visit and your continued support of our parish." I pulled the wooden door open with my left hand while gesturing my right hand outside. "And Father Oller is just one call away if I ever have any questions."

"We're not insinuating that you can't do it," Mr. Callahan said.

"Oh, of course not. I appreciate that you care," I said. "I appreciate both of you." My eyes bounced between the older couple.

"Well then. We'll see you this Sunday," Mrs. Callahan said before heading out.

"I'll see you then."

They marched to their car without looking back.

A gentleman wearing a black suit and white gloves opened the door of a black sedan, ushering the Callahans inside the car.

Jessica and I waved at the same time when they looked back. Their tight smiles couldn't cover the disappointment in their faces. *I hope I didn't upset them.*

"I'm so sorry about that, Father," Jessica said once we were inside. "They're very …" she paused, perhaps looking for kind words to describe our recent visitors. "Inquisitive," she finished with a chuckle.

Inquisitive. That was an understatement. "No need to apologize. I get it."

"Do you need anything else before I leave?" she asked.

THREE: THE PRIEST

"No, I think I'm okay."

The door creaked open, catching our attention once again. "Oh, thank goodness." Jessica placed her hand on her chest. "I thought it was the Callahans again." She blew out a breath when a tall man wearing a black sweatshirt and dark jeans entered the church. His head hung low, preventing us from getting a glimpse of his face. Wisps of blond hair sticking out of the hoodie covering most of his face was the only thing visible. He strode with intent to the confession booth, tugging the red velvet curtains with such vigor I thought it'd ripped from the hooks.

Jessica glanced at her watch. "Look at the time. It's already ten o'clock. Are you ready to start the confession hour?"

"I am." It was one of my favorite parts of being a priest. It was a great opportunity to gauge the community and come face-to-face with my flock.

"I'll leave you to it. Call if you need anything." She exited the church via one of the side doors leading to the rose garden.

I headed to the booth, going through the series of Bible verses I loved to employ for these kinds of visits. Most verses would work for most occasions. Stealing, infidelity, lying, guilt—you name it, there was a verse for it. "What has brought you here, my son?" I asked after settling on the cushioned seat.

The man lifted his head so quickly, his hoodie almost fell back. "Who the fuck are you?"

Four: The Reaper

The scent of spice and aftershave I'd come to know from Father Oller wasn't the one that greeted me when the curtains opened. Instead, the smell of fresh linen and oak filled the booth when someone who wasn't Father Oller took *his* seat.

"You're not him," I continued, leaning closer to the mesh separating our spaces. "Where's Father Oller?" I felt for the gun tucked into my waistband, my kill mode activated being caught off guard by this unfamiliar man on the other side of the confessional screen.

"He's gone to a different parish," the man with the baritone voice said. "I'm Father Saint James." His voice was too casual and sounded far too young to be a priest.

What the fuck? "Gone where? When?" I stood to leave. Why didn't Father Oller tell me he was leaving? I never would've come back had I known he was gone. He was the only reason I kept showing up at this place. Well, that and the comfort I received whenever I unloaded my sins on him. He was my savior, giving me a sense of hope, however false, that I would be redeemed. It'd been a while since my last confession, but he had delivered mass two Sundays ago and surely would've said something if he was leaving.

"Stay," Father Saint James urged. "He moved to the Philippines to fulfill his lifelong dream of leading a parish there," he explained. "Why don't you tell me your name?"

Like that was gonna happen. I'd been seeing Father Oller every month for years and he never once asked for my name. Not that I would tell him anyway. I had no name, and the one they called me required an explanation I would carry to my grave. "I am nobody," I said.

"Nobody?"

"Yes. Nobody."

"Okay," he said. "Why don't you tell me why you're here?"

My sight focused on the small window separating us and I couldn't help but notice his clean-shaven face. A set of red lips sitting on top of a cleft chin and square jaw. I didn't dare look him in the eyes. I never did with Father Oller because it was better that way. I sat back in the seat I had vacated seconds ago, debating whether I should stay or go.

"It's okay, my child. You're safe here."

My child. It sounded odd coming from him, but his voice was alluring, tempting the sins out of me—and heaven knew I had plenty. "In the name of the Father, the Son, and the Holy Spirit," I recited after kneeling. "It's been three months since my last confession."

It had been after my last assignment, which took me to Los Angeles. Confessing my sins to Father Oller after every kill had become as routine as the sunrise every morning, thinking it would wash away my wrongdoings. Who was I kidding? I was hopeless.

Pages were flipped on the other side of the wooden wall. Father Oller never used the Bible for me. He knew it by heart.

Seconds later, Father Saint James read a verse in the book of Matthew about forgiveness or some shit like that.

I'd heard that verse before, from Father Oller, who never recited the same verse twice. He always had something meaningful to deliver. Too bad it was all lost on me. "I killed two men," I confessed, cutting him off.

He was silent. The exact opposite of Father Oller's reaction when I first told him about the men I had killed. Against my better judgment, I chanced a look at Father Saint James's eyes.

He was staring back at me, but I couldn't decipher if the intensity in his eyes was that of shock, fear, or both.

My gaze traveled back to his lips. They were supple and moist, inviting me to devour them. I shook my head to get rid of those thoughts. That had come out of nowhere! I had enough sins, and lusting over the young priest was a recipe for disaster. My jeans became tighter, reminding me of how long it had been since I'd fucked a man. *Fuck!* The head of my cock was pressing the zipper of my pants through my boxers, rubbing with every shift in my seat. I adjusted my dick to the side, releasing a shallow breath once relieved of the building pressure.

"Why?" he asked.

I cleared my throat. "Huh?"

"Why did you kill them?"

"Because they would've killed me if I hadn't."

"And why would they want to kill you?" Another question. His eyes were still glued to me, perhaps judging.

"You're not supposed to ask all these questions." Father Oller had asked me why a couple of times, but stopped when he realized he wasn't going to get any answers. Not the real answers anyway. "You're supposed to offer prayer or ask me to repent."

"Do you repent killing these men?"

Another question. If I'd wanted an interrogation, I would've gone to ... well, I didn't know where I would've gone, but most definitely not here. Still, I thought about his question for a split second. *Do I repent killing?* I didn't. Maybe. There was no room for guilt and conscience with what I did.

We were taking down monsters. The worst of humankind. Those who got away without paying for their heinous crimes. The rapists, the human traffickers, the abusers, and the list went on. Our actions were justified.

"Don't be afraid," he said when I didn't answer.

"Sometimes."

I was shocked by my admission. I had to get the hell out before I said something I'd regret. I lived in shadows with secrets that would stay with me until my last breath. I didn't want to have to kill him like the others who'd had the misfortune of knowing too much. So, I bailed.

In a moment of introspection—the second I stepped out of the confessional—I realized that it was the way Father Saint James spoke that enamored me. The way his lips moved when he said *don't be afraid* had me sinning, adding weight to the cross I bore.

The resounding muted thud of my boots echoed through the empty building as I made my way out. Halfway through the door, I chanced a look behind me just as the maroon velvet curtain parted. I'd been right. He ducked out of the booth, revealing himself to be much younger than the former bishop. His blond hair was perfectly combed to the side of his head. He was as tall as me, with a slightly smaller frame. He nodded when he noticed my stare before disappearing into a room next to the booth, but not before I stole a glance of his muscular round ass. Who knew they made priests like that?

My red Harley motorcycle—one of the very few possessions I cared about—was where I'd parked it five blocks from the church. The priest had sparked a curiosity inside me and it needed to stop before it caught fire. After I pulled my black leather jacket from the bike's small storage compartment, I shrugged it on, and adjusted my hard dick before donning my tinted black helmet. I needed to come, and I knew where to find a wet mouth and a willing hole.

The engine vroomed when I turned on the ignition and twisted the right handlebar for more throttle. The noise was music to my ears. After maneuvering to the side of the road, I sped up with one goal in mind.

Club Z, Boston's last remaining bathhouse, hadn't changed since the last time I was there two years ago. This was the third time I'd stepped foot in this place because it offered nothing but a quick release. And just like the last time I was here, I was greeted by a dark hallway leading to a small counter with an old bulky computer screen that belonged in a museum. Next to it was a jar full of condoms. "Twenty-five to get in and another twenty-five to get a private room," the man behind the glassed-in counter said, leaning over and making a gesture of appraising me head to toe. "Yum." He clicked his tongue, making the most annoying sound imaginable.

I pulled my wallet out of my back pocket, fishing out a crisp fifty-dollar bill. Without uttering a word, I tossed the money on the counter and stuck my hand in the jar. With a fistful of foil wrappers, I picked the one labeled *XL* before tossing the rest back.

"Really?" the guy asked, staring at the foil packet in my hand.

FOUR: THE REAPER

"I'd do ya if I wasn't working." He mumbled something else, but I didn't care. I was here for one reason, and that reason was behind the door at the other end of the hall.

Techno music greeted me when I entered the dark room. The thumping house beat bounced off the walls illuminated by red lighting. Its only purpose was to dim the place. I hadn't made it past the entrance of the men's locker room—the *only* locker room—when someone completely naked blocked my way. I sized him up like he was my next meal. His body was glistening from the shower, his hair damp. His muscles were outlined by the shadows of the barely there lights and, judging by the size of his cock, he'd be a great fuck. Not that I cared, since I was there for my own release. Nothing more, nothing less.

Another man in the same state of undress came from behind him, grabbing his impressive bulge. They started kissing—no, tonguing—each other, while carnal sounds escaped their mouths. The smaller man shifted his gaze to me before whispering something to the other man.

They parted, came closer, and pushed me against the wall. Where that would usually freak me out, I let them.

One man groped me and the other licked the side of my neck while snaking his hand under my sweatshirt. "Hot!" he whispered, feeling the valley of my abs.

"You're so fucking hot, dude," the other guy said. He rubbed the length of my fully erect dick through my pants with his cheek, slowly unzipping my jeans. "I'm gonna suck you so good. You'll be dry by the time I'm done with you." He was on his knees looking up, eyes glossy with lust.

I shoved his face on my crotch. "Less talk, more action," I snarled.

The other guy slid his hand inside my boxers.

"Fuck!" I moaned. This was exactly what I needed.

"You like that, daddy?" he whispered, peppering my neck, ear, and cheek with kisses. His mouth moved to my lips.

I pushed him hard with one hand, and with my force and his size, he fell backward on the floor, his body sliding a couple of yards. "What the fuck are you doing?" I barked.

"The fuck, man, it's just a kiss," he said.

The bigger guy had stopped unwrapping his treat momentarily before freeing my cock from its confinement. "Hmmm." He moved his face closer to my crotch.

I pushed him away before he had a chance to engulf me, putting my dick back in my boxers, zipping my pants before running away. "Goddamn it!" It wasn't just a kiss. *No one gets to kiss me.* Fucking? I did that well. Kissing? No. Fucking. Way.

Five: The Priest

I hunkered deep in the transept of the church, my mind occupied by the unnamed man from the confession booth who had retreated moments ago. Just when I thought I'd heard them all, I was reminded once again how vile the world could be. I wasn't naive to think that men like him didn't exist. In fact, I knew they loomed in every corner of the city, walking among us daily. I'd witnessed it more times than I cared for. What I didn't expect was for someone to flat-out confess their sins and not feel a tiny bit of remorse about what they'd done. Quite often, the inner turmoil a person went through after committing a wicked act, an abominable cruelty, was palpable in their shaky voice, evident in their body language. But not him. *I killed two men.* He uttered those four words as if he was delivering the weather report.

Cool.

Calm.

Unaffected.

He was heavy on my mind minutes after he'd left in ways I couldn't fully comprehend. I headed out and sat on the marble bench situated in the middle of the rose garden, thinking about how someone so dangerous could live freely with the liberty to kill and come out unscathed.

Not my problem. I shook my head and rid myself of those thoughts, a rabbit hole I didn't have the luxury to dwell in, and focused my attention on the budding rose bushes surrounding me. The specs of color peeked out of their green buds, getting ready for their annual dramatic spectacle. Three days and three encounters later—with Father Oller, the Callahans, and the unnamed man—Boston was shaping up to be an epic mission. This assignment was one for the books and I was more than up for the task. A challenge I would take head-on, just like everything I'd done.

I wasn't always successful, but it had never stopped me from trying. I tapped my phone; a smiling image of ten-year-old me with my arms wrapped around my older brother's waist greeted me when it came to life. I didn't know it back then, or maybe it was my young mind failing to understand, but he'd been a father figure for my entire life. I scrolled through my call history and pressed Jessica's name.

"Father Saint James, hi. Is everything okay?" she asked, her tone laced with concern.

"Yes, everything is fine. I didn't mean to worry you."

"Oh, good," she said, exhaling with apparent relief. Jessica was a worrier—my very limited interactions with her had proved that—and I needed to find better ways to communicate with her without sounding the alarm. She might be the only person who liked me so far, and I needed her on my side.

"I'm going to head out and explore since I don't have anything left on my calendar today," I said. It'd been a while since the last time I stepped foot in the city I'd once called home. That was by choice. I wanted to prove to myself that I was worthy, and it had taken me more than six years and two parishes to get here. This mission was my redemption. And if I was about to spend a considerable amount of time in this town, I might as well get myself reacquainted with the city like an old friend. I needed its trust like my next breath.

"Well, that's lovely, Father." Her enthusiasm was back. "Check out the farmers' market between Dartmouth and Montgomery. It starts today and will last until fall."

"I might do that. Thanks again for all your help these past few days." Perhaps I could get her a small gift as a token of my appreciation. It wouldn't hurt to have an ally. God knew I could use one.

I stared at my phone after Jessica said goodbye, fighting an urge gnawing at the back of my mind. A burden I'd imposed on myself since I could remember.

Seconds passed and my thumb dialed a set of numbers I knew by heart, belonging to my older brother, Andrew. I hovered over the green call button. It had been a while since I'd called him, and my arrival in Boston brought to the surface a maelstrom of emotions I thought I'd buried in the darkest corner of my mind, a place where not even my heart could find.

Beep.

As expected, the call went straight to voice mail before the first ring. Out of habit, I cleared my throat and left a message. "It's me … again," I began, taking in a lungful of cool spring air to calm my shaking voice. "I'm back in Boston. I'm …" I paused, pinching the bridge of my nose. Images of him teaching me how to fight when I told him about the bully in grade school, of him guiding me while I navigated the ins and outs of the church flooded my brain like a reel on a loop. He was more than just my brother. He was my mentor. "I'm going to make you proud."

Andrew's mission in the Cathedral of Holy Cross had been cut short, only lasting a couple of years. He was given a more challenging mission after impressing his superiors and the Vatican. He left big shoes for me to fill. "I miss you."

I ended the message and stood. The weight I thought would've been lifted after the call never came. I was on my own. Perhaps they were right. Maybe I was too inexperienced for this mission. The voice in my head planted seeds of doubt, but I drowned it with Andrew's words: *You are made for this,* he used to say.

"Good morning, Father Saint James," Tim, the parish courier, greeted. He was distributing packages when I passed by him on my way to the bishop's house. Like me, he'd just moved to the city a few months ago and had only been with the church for three weeks.

"Good morning! Anything for me?" I asked.

Tim fingered through the stacks of envelopes painstakingly slowly before shaking his head. "Nothing yet, Father," he said. "Are you expecting something?"

"Nothing in particular," I answered, shaking my head.

"Maybe tomorrow."

I nodded and made my way inside the house. Strolling the city was sounding better and better by the minute. This could be good for me. After grabbing a light black jacket from the closet, I headed out and traveled by foot to the center of the city. Cherry blossoms were in bloom, their branches covered in pink cotton.

Two blocks into my walk, a young couple pushing a baby carriage stopped me. "Hi, Father," the woman greeted. "Aren't you Father Oller's replacement?" She pulled the cloth canopy open, revealing a newborn child.

"I am," I replied, offering my hand for a handshake. "Who do we have here?" I directed my attention to the baby swaddled in the carriage.

"This is our baby girl, Zoe. She was just baptized two weeks ago," the man answered, running his hand across Zoe's palm-sized head. Zoe wiggled at her dad's touch. Her eyes were closed and her cheeks were red.

"Hello, Zoe," I cooed to the sleeping child. "You have a beautiful family," I said to the couple.

"Thank you, Father. We'll see you on Sunday," the woman said, closing the carriage before walking away.

"Have a blessed day," I called. That encounter wasn't so bad, I thought, considering I was the replacement for the much-loved Father Oller.

"He's so young," the man whispered. He glanced back but immediately looked away when he met my eyes.

I spoke too soon. Somehow, I expected that comment before I heard it. Remarks like that were going to be part of my days going forward, and I had to get used to it. It was nothing personal, my age defied a tradition well established in our practice and custom.

I hadn't yet made my next step when an older lady stood in front of me, blocking my progress. "Is what I heard true? Are you the new bishop?" she asked.

"Yes, I'm Father Saint James."

She opened her mouth to say something when her cell phone rang. She frowned at the screen. The wrinkles on her face deepened. "I have to get this," she said before taking the call.

"Oh, please." I took it as a welcome opportunity to exit. A few more blocks in and several more interruptions later, I zipped my jacket all the way up to cover my black button-up shirt and white clerical collar, a neon sign advertising who I was and my role in the community. I didn't have a problem with crowds, nor engaging in conversation, but I wanted to explore the city and had a very limited time to do it.

The trick worked, since no one stopped me again. "Enjoy this," I murmured. These moments were numbered.

My eyes caught a glimpse of a dark shadow moving in my periphery, but it was gone the moment I looked. I searched around to see where it went, with no luck. I took a deep breath and relaxed the tension building on my shoulders, then continued perusing the city and getting lost in its beauty.

Aside from a couple of new modern skyscrapers, Boston appeared to be how I remembered it. Historic, colonial, brick-clad structures partially covered with ivies found harmony with contemporary glass buildings. Narrow cobblestone alleyways were steeped and preserved in their rich history. Copper sculptures stood in the middle of dozens of parks peppered throughout the city. Boston was stunning.

Rows of white tents greeted me when I cornered Montgomery Street. Jessica was right: this place was buzzing with activity. Stalls with products ranging from homemade candles and soaps to exotic spices lined three city blocks while people were engaged in conversations between the vendors.

The first booth, selling leather-bound notepads, snatched my attention. "Those are handmade," the man behind the counter said when I picked up one of the brown leather items.

"They're beautiful," I said, flipping it front and back. "Do you personalize?" I ran my finger over the engraving on the back of the notebook.

"With no extra charge," he answered, beaming. "My name is

FIVE: THE PRIEST

Zac."

"Nice to meet you, Zac," I said, matching his enthusiasm. The hair on the back of my neck and arms stood as a feeling of being surveyed washed over me. Slowly, I looked over my shoulder, searching, but once again found nothing but passersby and occasional bikers and runners sprinting along the sidewalk.

"I can do initials, names, or a verse up to twenty-five characters," Zac said, bringing my attention back to him and the soft leather-bound book in my hand. He maneuvered around, scooting into the narrow space between his and the neighboring stall. "Let me show you something," he said when he was standing next to me. He pulled back the tablecloth covering his worktable, revealing a selection of more leather goods in all shapes and sizes. He placed his glasses, which were hanging around his neck, back on before leaning over, searching the shelves. "There it is."

Zac's arm brushed mine as he explained about the distressed leather-bound notebook he'd pulled out from his hidden stash. "This is the best we have." He took my hand and brushed my fingers over the smooth surface. "Feel how soft it is. It's—"

He suddenly fell forward, facedown onto his booth before he could complete his statement. The force of his fall caused the table to roll further into his tent, hitting his cash register. He gripped the counter to brace his fall, but failed, pulling the black cloth down with him. Leather goods, coins, and bills scattered on the ground.

"Watch where you're going!" I called to the man who had caused the commotion. He was wearing a motorcycle helmet, seemingly unaffected by the bruteness of his action. The sunlight and clear blue sky reflecting on his tinted shield made it impossible to make out his face. "Sir, excuse me!" I called out again when he didn't look back. He didn't even stop.

I shook my head and brought my attention back to Zac, who was sprawled on the ground.

"Are you okay?" I offered a hand to help him to his feet.

"Yeah," he said, accepting my gesture. "That jerk pushed me." He pointed in the direction of the helmeted man.

A glint caught my eye. I crouched down and picked up Zac's glasses, which were laying near his feet. "They're broken," I said, passing him the bent frames and scratched lenses.

"Oh man. Asshole!" he yelled. I doubted the man heard him. He probably wouldn't care anyway.

I helped him gather up some of his items that had scattered on the ground. I was in disbelief about what had just happened and the lack of response from those nearby, as though it was the most mundane thing they'd ever witnessed. "I'll take two of these. The black one and the mahogany." I grabbed the two notepads and passed them to him.

"Do you want me to customize them?" he asked, checking the scratch across his forearm. He appeared somewhat recovered from his fall.

"Are you hurt?"

"A couple of scratches but I'll live." He winced when he pressed his index finger on his abrasion. "Now, let's not allow that dickhead to ruin our day. So, custom or not?"

Glad that Zac's spirit was back, I asked, "How long will it take? I don't have a lot of time." I didn't want to come back. If this was a normal occurrence in this part of town, count me out.

"Are you planning on walking around?"

I nodded.

"Good. It'll be done by the time you make your way back here." Zac handed me a pen and paper. "Write what you want here."

"I'd love that." I wrote three letters on the paper he handed me. "There," I said, handing it back to him.

"HSJ," he read out loud. "That's your initials?"

"Yeah."

"What's it stand for?" His Boston accent seemed to be getting thicker the longer I interacted with him.

"Heath Saint James." I handed him my credit card, waiting to see if he knew who I was. My arrival appeared to have spread like wildfire.

"That's your name?" He tapped my card onto his tablet before handing me the device to sign.

"The one and only," I joked, relieved that I didn't have to explain who I was and hear another *he's too young to be a priest* remark.

"I like that. Sounds fancy," he said. "Same initials for both?" He waved the two items in his hands.

"Let's leave the mahogany one blank."

He nodded. "I'll have these ready when you're done shopping. I'll throw in a free bookmark."

"Thank you, that's very kind." I headed to the next stall, where the delicious smell of artisan bread was coming from. I was hungry all of a sudden. The crowd parted for a split second, and there he was, the guy with the motorcycle helmet, facing my direction.

I darted toward him but a mob of people formed in front of me, meandering and blocking my view. I craned my neck to see if he was still there, but he was gone as fast as he'd appeared.

True to his word, my personalized purchase, including the complimentary leather bookmark, was completed when I rounded back to Zac's stall. "Thanks for this." I waved the bookmark at him before tucking it into one of the travel books I'd bought from the market and headed off, cornering the street.

A roar reverberated behind me and a speeding motorcycle zipped by my side. It was going so fast, all I saw was a flash of black. A couple more feet and it would have crashed into me.

"Whoa." I shook my head. *What a morning.*

Six: The Reaper

I hadn't planned on creeping up on the priest. But after my failed lay, my blue balls were about to fall off and that would be a tragic way to go. "What the fuck am I doing?" I asked myself. Answers flooded my brain but there wasn't one good enough for me to retrieve. It was too late anyway. I was nothing if not persistent. Plus, I doubted he would recognize me behind my tinted helmet shield.

Although, I must admit that a small part of me wanted him to know it was me.

The clown of a man selling the leather crap was lucky it was daylight and we were in public, because he would've been in the hospital wearing a full body cast had it been any other day. Was it too much? Maybe, but lessons had to be learned.

I made it to the priest's home minutes before him, since he walked to the center of town. I knew that too since I'd staked claim in front of his house, between two parked vans, after my interrupted fuck session at Club Z. I was patiently waiting for another glimpse of the priest to take with me when I jerked off. A sight of his face would have sufficed. But when he came out of his brick house, it was a no-brainer from there.

After giving the priest a few minutes—and a five-block head

start—I engaged in what I did best: tracking my target down like a predator hunting his prey. I stalked his every movement until he visited the last stalls.

I parked my bike in an alley behind the church. It was close enough to dash to in case of a disaster, but far enough away to stay out of sight. After setting a timer on my wristwatch, I jogged to the bishop's house. If my calculations were correct, like always, I had twenty minutes to spare before the priest made his way home. That would be enough time to find out more about Father Saint James.

A woman and a man who appeared to be around my age came out of the church, causing me to stop in my tracks. I turned my back on them as they neared me, sliding my leather gloves from my hands before tucking them in my pocket. They seemed to be unaware of my presence as they carried on their conversation.

"How do you like the new bishop?" the man asked.

"I like him. He seems very nice," the woman answered. "He's a little green, but he'll be okay."

Their voices hushed as they moved further away until their conversation evaporated. I glanced behind me just as they made their turn-off to the next street. I crept to the brick building matching the church's facade, canvassing the interior of the house through the glass windows before heading in the door. One twist of the knob let me know that it was locked, unsurprisingly. It was Boston, after all. Not even the holiest of places could escape the reality that men like me existed in the city.

I made my way to the backyard while keeping a close eye on the road and the church. It was past noon—in the middle of the week—and I doubted anyone was around. If there were people inside the church, the likelihood of them being tourists was high and they wouldn't know I wasn't supposed to be there.

Here we go. One of the windows by the kitchen was open halfway. And before pulling it all the way up, I checked behind me once again to make sure no one was nearby. I hoisted my body off the ground, thankful that the window frame held my two-hundred-and-ten-pound ass without breaking in half. Swiftly and quietly, I stretched my legs inside, one at a time, maneuvering into the house across the marble counter, while pausing and waiting for any hints of movement in between action. After several seconds passed and still no sign of anyone, I hopped off the counter, treading gingerly all the way to the living room with my back against the wall. I made my way to the window facing the church, separating the wooden blinds with my fingers to inspect outside before pulling them shut. Tiptoeing to the other side, I did the same with the ones facing the street.

Feeling somewhat secure, I moved around the house and stopped by the fireplace, where a photograph of the priest sat over the mantle. He stared back at me. I traced a gloved finger from his blue eyes to his red lips parted for a smile. I fished my cell phone out of my jacket pocket and snapped a couple of pictures before continuing my search.

My leg brushed an ottoman, causing it to slide out of place. It was a slight shift, but you never knew how much the priest would notice. I adjusted it back to where it was, making my presence as stealth as possible, leaving no trace of myself behind. Passing through a hallway adorned by a framed image of the Pope and a wooden cross, I made my way to one of the bedrooms and opened the closet in front of a well-made bed covered with decorative pillows. It was empty, with nothing but wooden hangers in it.

In the other bedroom, the larger of the two, I knew I'd found what I was looking for when a familiar scent greeted me. Like the other room, the bed was made but in a more functional way, without the exorbitant number of pillows occupying almost half of the surface. Behind me was a closet, twice the size of the one next door. I pulled it open, revealing a row of black shirts hung neatly on the left side of the wardrobe. Twelve of them, to be exact. To the right was a selection of ornate robes of different colors; white, green, purple, and maroon. Polished black leather shoes lined the floor of the closet, each pair placed about four inches from the next. A small wicker basket positioned against the wall had a couple of garments inside. I reached down and pulled a black shirt from the pile. It was the epicenter of the scent. I tugged the shirt to my nose, breathing in as much of Father Saint James as possible.

My watch vibrated, letting me know I had five minutes before the priest opened the door. A groan escaped my mouth while my cock stirred back to life from the visceral thrill of being caught and the urge to orgasm. I rolled the short-sleeve shirt up and tucked it into my pants before closing the closet door, leaving it the way I'd found it—minus the shirt. I zipped back to the kitchen, wiping the shoe prints off the countertop with my handkerchief, remembering to close the window halfway. I left out of the back door, keeping it locked as I walked out.

As expected, there was a rattling of keys at the front door about the same time the back door closed. I waited for a couple of minutes until the priest was inside before heading out to the street, ducking when I passed the windows.

A black SUV had been trailing me for a few blocks since I'd left the priest's home. I'd made a mental note of its license plate and had been keeping a close eye on it through my side mirror. It could well be my paranoia, but my gut was telling me otherwise. I twisted the throttle and sped up, curving a hairpin turn, riding my motorcycle against the traffic. Its deep rumble reverberated through the canyon of Boston's skyscrapers.

Horns blasted. Drivers cursed at my disregard for their safety.

Watching the black SUV through my mirrors, I saw it run a red light, which confirmed my suspicions.

After parking my motorcycle, I scrolled through my contact list and pressed Zero's name. She was one of the best hackers out there. I'd only spoken with her on the phone since her base of operations was in a remote mountain cabin in Vermont. "What's up, boo? Miss me already?" she asked when she picked up my call.

"I need you to run something for me." I made my way to the elevator of my apartment.

"What do you have?" Sounds of keyboard clicking carried through the receiver.

"Massachusetts license plate."

"Piece of cake. What is it?"

"2GR 712."

"Cool. I'll send it to El Jefe in the next thirty minutes," Zero said. "Is that fast enough?" I didn't know anyone who could hack into Boston PD's system that quickly.

"Actually, can you send it to me directly?" I held my breath, hoping she'd run this under the radar.

"I don't know, Reap. You're not doing anything shady, are you?" she asked, hesitation in her voice.

"No. It's personal," I answered.

"It always is. It always is."

"Is that a yes?"

"Yup. I'll text you."

"Thanks. Gotta go." The elevator opened to my floor. I hadn't made it to my unit when my phone buzzed with a text.

Zero: Plate's clean.

Me: K. Thanks.

I didn't know if that was a good thing or not.

I took my clothing off one piece at a time on my way to my bedroom until I was naked. With the adrenaline from this afternoon and the image of Father Saint James, I was all worked up. Silky pre-cum leaked from the head of my pulsating dick. There was no ignoring my painfully erect cock, and if I didn't come then, I would explode. I retrieved the priest's shirt and inhaled while cupping my hard-on, building a sense of rhythm. I made my way to the bed and sat on the edge. The urgent need to find release was overpowering. I brought the soft fabric to my face once more, closing my eyes and imagining him on his knees in front of me. I could smell him on me. He was nowhere and everywhere at once and I couldn't get enough.

I spit in my palm and mixed the saliva with pre-cum, sliding my fist over my swollen cock. My legs parted instinctively as I fantasized he was between them, licking my shaft. I cupped my balls, brushing across them as if it was his tongue.

This wouldn't take long; the pleasure built with every stroke. I wondered how good of a cocksucker he would be when I fed him every hard inch of what was in my hand. I stroked my cock harder and squeezed my sack at the same time. I loved receiving head, and wanted Father Saint James to bury his face in my crotch while I held his head against me, forcing him to accommodate every thrust.

The idea of him on his knees blowing me was the exact image I focused on as I continued to tug on the slick cock in my hand. The tension grew, my mind fixated on him struggling to take all of me into his skilled mouth. I rubbed harder, my dick sliding across his imaginary lips. He was in my control; I owned him. Two of my sexual favorites. My breath hitched as the sensation of my impending release overcame my desire for a protracted jerk session. This would not be a drawn-out event. I deeply inhaled his scent from the shirt, holding my breath, my fantasy expanding in my brain, stroke after gratifying stroke.

In my dreams, I reached for the back of his head and forced him on me just as I shot my hot load into his waiting mouth. I tensed as the orgasm spilled from me and into the emptiness of the room.

He'd been here, hadn't he? The mind could play tricks, especially when overtaken by pure and unadulterated lust. I'd been fooled by the piece of clothing in my hand, the fabric that had loaded my senses until I could hold off no more.

I collapsed on the bed, heaving, enjoying the post-orgasm bliss courtesy of my priest. I hadn't come that hard since ... I didn't fucking know, but I loved every second of it. I wondered if you could blackout from coming so hard?

My phone buzzed and I stood to grab it from my nightstand. A text from an unknown number appeared on the screen: *Pier 67 at sundown.* Without responding, I tossed my phone on the bed and headed to the bathroom.

The steam fogged the glass sliding door of the shower and the warm water cascading down my body resuscitated my dick. I lathered my hand with soap and stroked, Father Saint James in my head once again. Unlike the first round minutes ago, now I took my time, slowly dragging my palm from the base to the tip of my soapy cock. I never denied having a high sex drive. I liked it a lot, so I sought it out when the need to get off rattled my brain. And even though I'd just orgasmed minutes before, I was always ready if the mood struck. Simply soaping my balls and rubbing a finger over the taint just behind them had me at full mast again, images of the priest still haunting my desires.

This time I'd try to take my time, let my vivid imagination conjure up another hot scene of me dominating the man in my psyche. He'd been disturbing me, causing my cock to ache in pain—I wanted to use him so badly. I slid my hand down my shaft and squeezed the head of my dick, rubbing it intensely until the sensation was too much. The soap acted as the perfect lubrication to my self-assault. What dirty deed did I want the *man of God* to do to me this time?

The mirage in the shower mist turned away from me and placed his hands on the foggy glass. Water cascaded over him as he spread his legs, the spray gathering on his back and falling toward his ass crack. I watched as the water disappeared into the place I wanted to stick my cock. I stroked faster and kept my eyes closed, watching his ass tease me. He thrust his ass backward, begging me to fill him. The urges exploded in my mind yet again, as though I hadn't come only minutes ago.

I rode the dream state further, even though Father Saint James had his hooks in me—something I never allowed—but right now he was all about milking the next load out of me. His smooth and athletic ass begged for me to enter him right there in the shower. My soapy hands squeezed my balls painfully in an attempt to push the need away from my thoughts. I had a man to fuck and he was bending over alluringly in the misty enclosure. My pace quickened.

I built up lather on my cock and kept my focus solely on the forbidden fruit of Father Saint James. I swore he actually turned around and glanced from my eyes to his asshole. "Fuck me," his ghost mouthed. My cock flexed in anticipation.

Just the idea of filling his ass with my tool became too exciting for me to last. It was already too late. My shaft stiffened as I felt my load shooting out of me. I'd tried hard to work this one out nice and slow but failed again—because of him.

I'd even left his shirt on the bed, yet it hadn't mattered. He was everywhere. He'd become everything I thought of when the urges arrived. How long would it be before I could no longer accept the visualization and had to possess the real Father Saint James?

***

I spotted him right away. The man was sitting on a bench, facing the water, unmoving. The sun was setting and a small crowd had gathered at Pier 67 to watch the sun disappear behind the city, leaving a burst of red, orange, and blue saturating the sky. I'd been watching him from afar, monitoring the perimeter, making sure he was by himself, and after the dark sky had settled and the crowd thinned into a handful of people, I walked toward him, glancing around to make sure I wasn't being followed. Paranoia had been wreaking havoc on my calculated life and I despised it.

I sat on the opposite side of the bench, facing the city. We were side by side and neither of us looked at each other. Silence lingered for a brief moment before he spoke. "The view is better down here than where you were," he said. "You didn't have to keep me waiting."

"I don't trust you," I said. It was nothing personal, but I didn't trust anyone with what I was doing. Especially when I wasn't sure myself.

"Then why am I here?" He shifted on the bench and my hand immediately traveled to the weapon at my waist.

"Relax," he whispered. "I'm on your side. You know that, right?"

I chuckled. There was only one person on my side. *Me.* And some days, even I doubted that. "What did you find?" I asked.

Tobias—otherwise known as The Savior—glanced at me, his gaze lingering for a while.

"What?" I asked through gritted teeth, meeting his stare. He was a handsome man, in a rugged kind of way. Older than I was, maybe late thirties or early forties. His light brown hair was buzzed close to his scalp. I couldn't see his eyes; he was wearing sunglasses despite the lack of sun. A little clichéd but whatever.

Tobias must've read my mind. He took his shades off and rested them on his near-bald head. His light brown eyes studied me with intensity. He was the first to break eye contact, pulling a white envelope from his coat pocket, leaving it on the space he vacated when he stood. "I'll contact you when I know more," he said before walking away. He stopped after five steps. "Be careful out there," he added without looking back. He placed his sunglasses back on before disappearing into the shadows.

I stood and grabbed the packed-to-the-brim envelope, clear tape keeping the contents from falling out. What the hell was in this thing? I couldn't risk opening it in public. Not with everything that had been happening lately. After tucking them in the waistband of my pants, right next to the gun, I pulled my hoodie back over my head and walked three blocks to my bike.

I rode to an abandoned warehouse ten miles north of Boston, squeezing my way through a slit of an opening in the wire fence, leading to a maze of empty shipping containers stacked in fours. I probed around the perimeter before my feet led me all the way back to a nondescript rusted container.

The padlock popped open when I slid my key in the lock. Once inside, I ripped the envelope open. It was a stack of images, taken from a distance judging by the pixelation and granularity. Even with the somewhat poor quality, I was able to make out some of the faces. Senator John Evans was in every frame, and according to the time stamp on the images, these photos were taken before he was assassinated on his way to a press conference eight months ago.

I flipped through the photos. Every still image moved like a reel as I went through them one by one, searching for any signs of The Firm's blueprint. The Firm never claimed the hit, but my instinct was telling me otherwise. Not even El Jefe could deny nor confirm his assassination.

My eyes started to hurt, my head felt about ready to split in half from pain. "Fuck!" I threw the photos against the iron wall in frustration. *What am I missing?*

Seven: The Priest

The sound of knocking coming from the front door woke me from one of the best sleeps I'd had since arriving in Boston. Still immersed in my vivid dream, it took a second for my foggy brain to register where I was and that the encounter I was having was, in fact, just a dream. I reached for my phone on the nightstand to check the time and whined. The screen turned black, allowing me to see my reflection. My forehead was soaked with sweat, while wet hair formed locks on the sides of my head. My whole body was damp.

I looked down at the tent of fabric caused by my erection, evidence of the wild dream I'd had about the unnamed man in the confession booth yesterday. He was all over me, kissing and nipping at my neck, his hands under my robe, pulling my underwear down in one swift move. He pushed my abdomen until my back was against the wall. His mouth neared the head of my shaft, but I was woken before I felt the warmth of his lips enveloping me.

It wasn't the first time I'd thought about a man pleasuring me.

My pulse raced with recollection. My younger years had

validated my attraction to men. I even went as far as dipping my toes in the water, having sex with guys when I was in college. But that was in the past. Any thoughts of intimacy had to be eradicated from my mind to be worthy of my calling. Being a priest was first and foremost in my life. Anything else would have to take a back seat, or be forgotten altogether, if I was to succeed. And now that I'd made it here, failure was not an option. Not again. I'd deprived myself of pleasure for so long, I'd all but forgotten how it felt. Even my dreams made sure I'd never experience it.

Knock. Knock. Knock.

A succession of three softer knocks drew me out of my thoughts. Who was here at five in the morning? Jessica never mentioned an early appointment, and I wasn't expecting anyone. It couldn't be the cleaners, since they came in yesterday while I was out. Or at least I thought they had—why else would the furniture and framed photograph be out of place? I'd always been a morning person, but five o'clock was way too early.

Another knock, louder this time, wiped the last remnants of sleep from my head and I scurried to grab my house coat. The smooth fabric snagged on my fully erect cock. I stood still, summoning the least sensual image I could imagine in hopes of getting my erection under control. It failed, so I gave up trying. "Coming," I said, shivering as my bare feet crossed the chilled floor. I turned the living room lights on, and when I did, the rapping stopped.

No one was outside the door when I opened it. Only silence and the cold morning air welcomed me. I looked left and right; I momentarily questioned if the knocking had actually happened or if I was in the middle of another dream.

"Hello?" My call went unanswered. As I stepped out the door to get a better view of the street, I trod on something slippery. What on earth? I tightened the belt on my robe before bending over to reach beneath my foot. It was an envelope. I glanced around one last time before heading inside.

I was all out of sorts. I slapped my cheeks to urge my brain to wake up and catch up to what was happening. The envelope was sealed, blank and surprisingly warm. I flipped it over to find two words: *The Bishop*.

I ripped open the envelope and a small thumb drive fell into my hand. It was also warm, as though it was just pulled out of a port. My curiosity growing, I headed to my office and fired up my laptop. It would take a while for the welcome screen to appear, as it had been a good minute since the last time I'd used it. Four days, to be exact, when I'd left Albuquerque.

Coffee. I needed coffee. I shuffled to the kitchen to brew a pot. Movement at the window caught my attention. I spun, and the pot fell from my hand, clamoring loudly in the sink. A person was there, peering inside. Goosebumps covered my body, an unsettling feeling taking residence in my mind. I grabbed a knife from the magnetic strip on the backsplash and ran to the front door, walking around the house to check the perimeter. But, just like before, no one was there.

"Now I really need coffee," I murmured.

Feeling somewhat awake after two full cups and the rush of adrenaline, I slid the drive into my laptop's USB port.

A pop-up notification appeared on the screen, prompting for a password. I reached over and fished the discarded envelope from the wastepaper basket. "What's the password?" I whispered. I ripped it open to check if there was a clue inside.

SEVEN: THE PRIEST

Nothing.

I stared at the screen and entered passwords I'd used in the past, but none of them worked. After three failed attempts and the fear of being denied access altogether, I pulled the thumb drive out. My mind raced at a million miles per hour. Stress was building in the muscles of my shoulders and neck, and that was my mark to stop. I massaged the back of my neck to release the building tension. Since there was no going back to sleep, I headed back to my room, put on sweats, and headed out for a run.

The sun was an hour from rising and the crispness in the spring air shrouded the city in a thick mist. I stood for a moment, adjusting to the chill. There, again—a person appeared on the road ahead of me. A man. He was wearing a baseball cap, which cast shadows over his features, making it impossible for me to make out his face. With his stillness and the graying fog surrounding us, he looked like the outline of an unfinished painting.

One of the streetlamps flickered, catching my attention. When I returned my gaze, he was gone. "Hello?" I ventured, tentative at first but then again, louder. Nothing.

It wasn't the first time I'd felt a presence watching over me, and sometimes I questioned my sanity. I shook my head and brought my hands to my mouth, blowing warm air onto them. My feet took the lead from my brain and I set off, unaware of where I was heading. I didn't mind. I was consumed by two thoughts: What was in the file, and who was the man?

Two men broke through the fog, heading in my direction. They were whispering, but I couldn't make out their conversation. I checked the street name to figure out where I was and groaned. I'd been so deep in my head I hadn't realized that I'd stumbled into the sketchiest part of town. I pivoted away from the men but it was too late. They ran to stand in front of me.

"Excuse me," I said, trying to move past them.

"What's the rush?" One of the men grabbed my elbow. "Empty your pockets," he said. His grip tightened, his face inches away from mine. His breath smelled like alcohol and the worst case of halitosis imaginable.

"Look, I'm just passing by," I said, my eyes bouncing between them. They were filthy. Their hair was clumped by what I could only assume was dirt. Their faces were covered with dust, while their clothes were soiled. Foul odor permeated from them.

"I said empty"—*hiccup*—"your pockets," the man slurred.

"I don't have any money," I said.

"How 'bout your phone?" the other man asked.

"I don't have my phone with me," I said. It occurred to me these men might be armed.

The man holding my elbow twisted my arm behind my back while the other aggressively searched my pockets.

"I told you, I don't have anything." I winced as my arm was twisted higher.

"What's this?" A hand withdrew from my pocket—he'd found the USB drive. I'd forgotten I had it. The man waved it in my face. His bloodshot eyes were glassy. These men were not just drunk. They were under the influence.

I squirmed. "They're just files. I don't want to get anyone hurt. Let me go."

Unsatisfied with my answer, he grabbed the collar of my sweatshirt, firm despite his inebriation. "Give us your money or—"

SEVEN: THE PRIEST

He wasn't able to complete his threat. A man in a black hoodie yanked him back and swung his fist into his face, and the thug landed cold on the ground.

"Who the fuck are you?" the guy holding my arm asked. He thrust his free hand, which was now holding a knife, toward the hooded man. "Get the fuck outta here," he screeched, waving his weapon. "Go!"

The hooded guy grabbed his knife-holding hand and bent it with force. A blood-curdling scream followed the sickening snap.

I jumped away when he released me.

"My hand!" he wailed, falling to his knees.

The other guy stirred, consciousness slowly returning. He sat up when he saw his buddy's busted wrist. "The fuck?"

"I'd run if I were you." The hooded guy's voice was deep and familiar. *Oh.* How could I forget? He was the subject of the very sinful dream I'd not long ago woken up to.

The thug didn't have to be told twice. He scrambled to his feet and disappeared into the fog in a heartbeat. *Some friend.* The wailing man stumbled as he got up, staggered back, and took off after him.

The hooded man stood in front of me. Without uttering a word, he examined my hand. His touch was surprisingly tender and caused chaos in my already messed-up state. He caressed my wrist; the sensation was so strange and unfamiliar I pulled it back.

"I'm okay," I whispered. "But I don't think he is," I added, cocking my head in the direction of the assailants. That wrist was definitely broken, with torn tendons to match.

"They're lucky I held back," he said, turning away. The instance of our first meeting flooded my brain. *This man knows how to kill.*

"What's your name?" I asked.

To my dismay, he didn't answer. He continued walking away, in time for the first ray of sunrise.

"Thank you," I called, but I doubted he heard me. I looked down and touched the part of my hand where we'd connected.

Eight: The Reaper

I slid a wooden hanger a quarter of an inch to the right to match its distance from the rest of my hanging clothes. Keeping things tidy and in place was peace for me. And with the chaos and darkness seeping through many facets of my life, I found peace however and wherever I could.

I combed my closet full of black clothes for something to wear—unnecessarily, I knew—before settling on a black hoodie, black jeans, and black leather jacket. Selecting was easier when you had one color palette to choose from. I tucked my gun into my waistband before heading out to meet El Jefe for my new assignment.

I preferred riding my bike, but it had been raining steadily for the past few hours so I opted to drive my Jaguar F-Type coupe—black, of course. The windshield wipers worked overtime to keep up with the torrential rain. I turned on the satellite radio and tuned in to my go-to news station. "This just in," the female broadcaster announced. "An explosion in Havana was reported this afternoon, and a Cuban news outlet has confirmed one fatality. We reached out to local authorities for comment, and here is what the Chief of Havana Police said to the press."

What the fuck? Using the control on the steering wheel, I raised the volume. *"Todavía estamos investigando el evento y le haremos saber a todos ustedes una vez tengamos una respuesta concreta,"* the chief said.

I paid close attention, my very limited Spanish being put to the test, glancing between the road and the console. I hoped they'd translate what the chief said.

That's it? Who fucking died?

The announcer continued. "According to police, they are still investigating the bombing and don't yet have any concrete information to share."

I switched stations in search of a more thorough report, but aside from football and scheduled programming, there was nothing about the Havana explosion. "Damn," I whispered.

Dread took up residence in my head, the gloom outside matching my frame of mind.

All eyes were on me when the elevator opened to the thirteenth floor of our office. Nobody knew this floor existed outside of The Firm. There was no button for this floor and it could only be accessed using an electronic keypad programmed to stop on the unluckiest number of them all. Stares followed my every move until I made it to the bulletproof glass door.

One of the men sitting behind the gray marble counter picked up a receiver, still staring. He spoke quietly, but I lip-read him saying *"He's here"* to the person on the other end. He ended the call and typed something into a tablet. Seconds later, the locks clicked and disengaged.

I made my way inside El Jefe's dark and dreary office, plunking my ass wordlessly on one of the seats in front of his desk. A dim floor lamp behind him provided the only

EIGHT: THE REAPER

light.

I tapped my phone screen and brought up the photo of Father Saint James. He'd occupied my mind since I stepped out of his confession booth, to the point of heading back to his house for another glimpse of his face. I was glad I did. He could've been seriously hurt if I hadn't been around. The notion made my blood boil. I looked down at his smiling face to keep my rage at bay. The things I wanted to do with those lips of his, wondering how my name would sound in his mouth when he screamed as he came, after I'd taken him over the edge time and time again. There was no place for my wild thoughts about him, but here we were. How could someone so holy be so sinful? If there was any doubt I'd end up in hell, I had just punched myself a one-way ticket to sinner's land.

A thud brought me out of the insane fantasy. El Jefe had dropped a thick folder on the oak desk. "Your next assignment," he said, pointing to the file. He stood and moved to the floor-to-ceiling glass windows, pulling a packet of cigarettes from his suit jacket. The red and orange sky in front of him was slowly fading to blue and black.

"What is it?" I asked, watching him flick the metal lighter.

He was quiet and that was something coming from him. He always had something to say, even if our conversations were one-sided.

I shoved the folder into my bulletproof backpack and studied him. "Who was it this time?" I asked, knowing that the only time he got this silent was when one of our men's assignments failed. Which for us meant death.

"One of our operatives was killed in Havana today. It wasn't during an assignment either," he said, staring at the city below. The stuffy room filled with tobacco smoke.

"The bombing?" I asked.

He nodded. "You heard about it?"

"On the news on my way here. Who was it?" Knots formed in my stomach. Billowing anxiety threatened to swallow me whole. The dread I felt when I heard the news on the radio was back, only this time with a vengeance.

He took another drag of his cigarette. "The Surgeon was ambushed on his way to the hotel."

No! It was as if someone had dumped a bucket of icy water on me. My whole body tensed, and I balled my hands. "William?" I whispered.

El Jefe blew out a breath. "Yes." His back was still to me.

What the fuck? Was it the same fucker who'd sent those clowns after me? I couldn't think. I could barely breathe. Forcing myself to take steady breaths, I schooled my expression. Life was a game of poker I'd mastered early on. Never show anyone what you were dealt. Not what's in your hands, never on your face, and definitely not in your actions. That was a lesson I'd learned the hard way.

"How well did you know him?" he asked, turning to face me. "The Surgeon." He moved to his desk and flicked glowing ash from the tip of his cigarette into the round crystal tray on its edge. The moonlight cast shadows on his face, hardened by the lives we lived. He watched me for a while, awaiting my response. "So? How well did you know him?" he repeated when I didn't answer.

"Well enough to fuck him," I answered, hoping that my agitation was masked by my indifference. We never fucked. We'd been tempted, but realized we were better off as friends. We were the closest both of us had to family. I stood, suddenly needing to get the hell out. I couldn't let El Jefe see how The

EIGHT: THE REAPER

Surgeon's death had affected me. *Fuck!* It would be the last time I'd let myself care for anyone.

The automatic door of his office clicked as I was about to turn the knob. "Let me go," I grumbled when the door didn't open. "I said let me go!" I turned to face him. Surprisingly, none of his minions rushed into the room. What a shame; in this mood, I wanted to bust some faces and break some jaws.

His hand was under his desk, where I knew the control for his door was, keeping me hostage. "Not until you tell me what happened in Havana," he demanded. His bleak features seemed more drastic, deep lines carved in his forehead, dark circles around his eyes. It was subtle, but his voice broke when he spoke. He cared for his men, but, like me, he'd been an expert at hiding his feelings away—like a wise and seasoned poker player. I learned from the best. "Who's hunting our operatives? What's in Havana?" he asked.

"I told you. I don't know." I turned my back on him once again. "Open the door."

"Everyone who gets close to you ends up dead."

His statement would've stung, but my heart was hollow and emotions were a sign of weakness. Also, what he said was true.

"Archer!" he called. He was one of the very few people who knew my real name and I liked to keep it that way.

I looked back and met his stare. "I don't know." That wasn't a lie. I *didn't* know who was hunting us. Havana was the place William and I would go to escape our crazy lives, even if it was temporary. It was our secret hideaway. *Not so secret after all.*

He studied me for a while before pressing the control. The lock disengaged. "After this assignment"—he pointed to my backpack—"find out who's hunting our men. And trust no one."

With my hands firmly in my jacket pockets, I stormed out of El Jefe's office. My vision tunneled to the swanky elevators with glossy wooden finish, passing through the sterile lobby posing as an interior design firm. It was a coverup to hide the gruesome truth behind the glass and metal doors.

The men and women manning the desks were skilled mercenaries hoping for their chance to be part of the operatives hired to 'right the wrongs' and serve justice to those citizens influential and wealthy enough to pay themselves out of crimes they committed. They might have dodged the system unscathed, but one way or the other, justice had to be served. That was where we came in. We were a group of trained assassins with history tracing back to the beginning of World War II. It was a privilege passed down through generations; or maybe it was a curse, some days I wasn't sure. We kept the balance. We were told from the beginning. But lately, I wasn't sure anymore.

The elevator door opened, the mirrored walls hiding dozens of cameras mounted with precision to capture vantage points of everyone within its confinement. I had no doubt El Jefe was watching me through their lenses. I remained collected, pressing the L button twice to close the door so I could get the fuck out of this place. Once outside, I flipped my collar up and marched to my car.

"William," I whispered, sliding the window open for a dose of fresh air. Spatters of rain dropped on my face. *Who did this to you?* It was true what they said about people like us. We lived in the shadows, surrounded by death and devoid of hope.

EIGHT: THE REAPER

I reached over and pulled the glove box open, riffling through leaves of papers until I found it: an old photograph of The Surgeon. He was grinning, something he did a lot. I used to find it odd how he was able to find a reason to smile. He was serene in this sea of utmost despair. William didn't belong to our world because he was nothing like us. Whoever killed him had to be good. William was meticulous. His actions were calculated. He moved with accuracy and precision, just like a surgeon.

I grabbed the golden lighter resting on the console of my car, flicking it to life. The amber flame danced in the breeze, pulling William's image like a magnet. I held the photograph over the flame, thinking about his voice and his memory until every surface of his smiling face turned to ash. "I'll miss you, my friend," I said, tossing the charred photo into the air, drifting away with the rain as it faded to nothingness. A fitting end for us. Because we were no one. "There will be no one to mourn us when we die. No family. No friends," William once told me.

Well, friend, I will mourn you. "You're at peace now. Till we meet again."

I settled into the seat of my car. Rage brewed within me. *Your death will not be in vain. I will find who did this to you. They will pay.* After allowing myself a brief moment to feel, I pushed start and the car roared to life.

Speeding through the streets of Boston, I blasted the stereo. The beat of the bass matched the one in my chest. I needed a distraction, and I knew where to find it. My car took me to a familiar place. I wasn't there to pray, nor to confess my sins. I was there to fulfill a growing appetite. My craving for the forbidden. Someone I shouldn't have. But with the shit

I'd just gone through tonight, forbidden was exactly what I needed.

Nine: The Priest

Three Years Ago

Layers of unsettling emotions multiplied within me as we neared the door. The glee of having my brother, Andrew, around was being replaced by a pining melancholy, knowing it would probably be years before we saw each other again. Life was unpredictable that way. We were inseparable when we were younger and never thought we'd spend most of our adult lives thousands of miles apart. I'd missed him.

"Are you sure you can't stay?" I asked him on our way to the car that was waiting to take him to the airport. His visit had been a surprise and I was elated when he showed up on my doorstep that morning. Thankful that it was midweek and I didn't have to deliver a mass, we spent most of the day together. It'd been a while since we'd seen each other, and I needed him now more than ever: his guidance, his support, his love.

A tight smile graced his face before he shook his head. Andrew was ten years older than me, but he looked a lot older than thirty-seven. The sides of his head showed specks of gray, and new wrinkles appeared on his forehead and around his eyes. They weren't there when I saw him two years ago after graduating from the seminary. "I wish I could, Heath, but my flight leaves at five," he said.

I glanced at my watch, willing the hands to stop turning, for time to stand still so I could have more moments with my brother. I had so many questions only he could answer. My reassignment in San Felipe, Albuquerque, started a few months ago. It was exactly what I thought it would be at the beginning, but lately I'd been questioning if I was the right bishop for the mission. I'd only been out of school for two years and it showed.

"Are you okay?" I asked, feeling guilty that I had made this visit all about me.

"I'm fine," he answered. "You can do this." Andrew must've sensed my distress hidden in my silence. He'd always been great at seeing through me. Sometimes, I wondered if he knew me better than I knew myself. He seemed like he could read my mind—back when we were younger and especially now. "You've worked your entire life for this."

"What if I fail?" My voice broke at the reminder of my time at San Luis Obispo months ago. "Again." This was a side of me only he could see. I didn't have to be strong all the time around Andrew. I didn't need to have all the answers when I was with him. I could fail with him without the fear of being reprimanded and shamed.

Andrew stopped walking. He looked around the church, perhaps to make sure that no one was around. "That was different. You weren't ready then. But you are now. Leave the past behind."

"I sometimes wonder if I'm cut out for this life." I didn't mean to say it out loud, but it was too late to take it back. I dared not look in his eyes, fearing to see disappointment in them.

He studied my face before he spoke. "You're born to do this, Heath. Don't let one hiccup derail your future. It's in the past and there's nothing you can do to change that. What matters is right now." He pulled me close, wrapping his arms around me. Priests weren't huggers, but we were brothers first. "You need to be kind to yourself.

Sulking will not get you anywhere."

I hugged him back tighter.

"Remember what the uncles used to tell us?" he asked.

I nodded. "Keep your eyes on the prize."

"That's right. I'm sorry that happened, but I believe in you. I always have." He released me from his embrace and placed my face between his palms, urging me to look him in the eyes. "I'm just one call away, brother."

"Okay," I said. "Thank you."

"I have to go." He kissed the top of my head before closing the short distance between me and the door.

I nodded and watched him exit the cathedral. You're born to do this. *Andrew's words replayed in my head moments after he was gone.* "I hope you're right." *How could I forget the past when there was always something to remind me of it?*

***

Three hours and ten failed login attempts later, I'd given up. I leaned back in the swivel chair, looking up at the ceiling. I rubbed my eyes; my eyelids felt like they were made of fine grains of sand, dry from staring at my computer screen for most of the day. Memories of the morning flooded my brain. I could've handled the situation with the two drunk guys mugging me myself. I was just buying time—until the man in black interrupted with his savage skills. How did he even know I was there? I thought he might have been the same man creeping around the house this morning, but the guy in the shadows was leaner and wore a cap, while the hooded guy was muscular and tall.

I stretched my arms over my head, yawning. After waking

up in the manner I did and the stress of my encounter, I was beat. Maybe a shower would perk up my spent body and recharge my fried mind.

I ignored the grumbling of my stomach and went straight to my ensuite bathroom. I turned the shower to hot, stripping until the water warmed up to my liking. I headed out to the hamper in my closet to deposit my dirty clothes and paused. It appeared to be missing a shirt, the one I had worn the other day. I counted the number of garments in the basket and started to question my wits. "I need to calm down," I murmured, closing the closet door. I pulled my robe from the back of the sofa on my way back to the bathroom.

The steam of the spray had already fogged up the room, and I stood in front of the round mirror, wiping the moisture from it. *I'm just tired*, I told myself, staring at my reflection. It had been a stressful few days, but everything would be okay. While others were convinced I was the best priest for this mission, it wasn't in my nature to believe it. Especially after two questionable results. I'd been close both times, but close didn't count—not in my world. That was the painful truth. There had to be a reason for my presence back here. My superior needed to tell me now.

***

A Week Ago

The unnatural silence of the hallway leading to the room where an archbishop from the Vatican was waiting to meet with me was eerie, adding dread to the outcome of this impromptu 'visit.' Was it too late to turn around? I wished Andrew was here to guide me.

NINE: THE PRIEST

This was the second time I'd had the misfortune of being at the receiving end of a 'visit,' but the way one of the red-robed deacons urged me to keep walking when I stopped to look back meant the choice wasn't entirely up to me, if I had a choice at all. So I nodded and kept my pace. My hands were shaking and my palms were sweating.

"Close the door behind you," Archbishop Lloyd said when I entered his office. I was relieved to see it was him. It felt like a lifeline had been thrown at me knowing he would be the one to deliver my verdict. Archbishop Llyod was a family friend. He knew my uncles very well, and he was my brother Andrew's mentor.

"It's you." A sigh of relief escaped my mouth as I reached behind me to close the door.

"Yes, Father Saint James. How long has it been since the last time I saw you?" he asked, motioning to the chair. The regalia of rings on his hands denoted his rank within the church.

"It would be nine years," I said, and occupied the seat in front of his ornate desk. "On my twenty-first birthday."

"That's right. I forget how young you are." He flipped the folder stamped with the gold Vatican insignia in front of him, revealing documents with the word CLASSIFIED watermarked all over them. "I asked them if I could deliver the news to you," he said, as though he was reading my mind. "And they agreed. Considering ..."

Considering his connection with my family. I remained quiet, anxious to hear what was coming next. Although I'd expected his visit, it didn't make what he had to say easier to swallow.

"I owe that to your uncles. God bless their souls." He signed the cross before continuing. "And your brother, Andrew."

"Have you heard from him?" I asked. Hearing his name threatened to tear my heart apart. He had been missing for months, during his stay in Texas. No one had heard from him, and I refused to believe anything but that he was alive. He was all I had.

"I haven't, son." He shook his head. "Upon negotiating with our connection at the Vatican ..." He paused before pulling my files from the folder. "They are willing to put everything that happened behind." He produced a lighter from his desk drawer and flicked it to life, catching the edge of the papers on fire.

My eyes bounced between the Archbishop and the burning papers. "Everything?" I asked in disbelief.

"Everything." A knowing look graced his face, and I knew a condition would soon follow. This was the Church, after all. Nothing was given without something in return.

"What do I have to do to redeem myself?" I asked, hopeful at the prospect of a third chance.

"It's time for you to go back home, Father Saint James." He tossed the blazing pile into the metal bin, where they continued to smolder until all that was left was singed sheets and embers. "This mission is your redemption. Your chance to prove that you are one of us. Can you do that?"

"Just tell me what I need to do and I will do it," I said.

"That's the spirit." He leaned back, straightening his embellished robe. "Everything is set for your transfer. You're leaving in two days." His lips pulled back into an ominous smile. I trusted that he wasn't planning anything sinister when it came to me, but he still made me uneasy. But if Andrew trusted him, I should too.

"You want me to move from Albuquerque to Boston in two days?" Where would I live? What about my belongings?

"Yes. We'll give you more details when you're settled." He stood and headed to the door. "There's nothing for you to worry about."

"Wait—you had everything arranged before I even said yes?" I asked. "Don't I have a choice?"

"Choice is an illusion, Father Saint James." He stopped walking,

NINE: THE PRIEST

but he didn't look back at me. "It's a mirage. They like us to believe we have a say, but our future is determined the moment you put on your robe for the first time. We don't have a choice."

"Andrew did," I said. "You did."

The archbishop glanced at me, shaking his head. "You're young. You have so much to learn. It would be a shame if your quest ends here." He opened the door, signaling that this meeting was over. "Don't blow this chance. Andrew wouldn't want you to," he whispered near my ear as I passed him. He knew what he was doing. "Only you can do this mission."

I turned to speak, but Archbishop Lloyd had already shut the door.

***

I shook my head to rid myself of thoughts of Archbishop Lloyd and focused on what Andrew used to tell me. *You're born to do this.* I thought about my training and all the sacrifices I'd made. I couldn't go back now, it was too late.

"You're not a failure and your career isn't over," I told the man in the mirror. And if I had to delude myself into thinking otherwise, I had to keep my eyes on the mission alone. One day at a time. The conclusion of my legacy depended on this assignment. *I am worthy of being a priest.*

I nodded to myself and took a deep breath. I pulled the shower glass door open and stayed under the spray of warm water for a long time, washing away the day's worries.

Tomorrow was a brand-new day.

Ten: The Reaper

Security spotlights lit up the church, while the wall of cherry blossom trees cast shadows on the bishop's home, cloaking it under darkness. The rain had stopped, but the shushing of the wind remained. The church appeared deserted, but it still took me a minute to find a perfect place to park, a site giving the optimal view of Father Saint James's bedroom. My wheels skidded to a stop when a spot opened across the street, parallel from his house. From the road, the lights on the bishop's house were off. That was odd, considering it wasn't late in the evening. He could be out and about, or sleeping, both options shouldn't make a difference to what I was aiming to accomplish.

I killed the engine and hopped out of the car to secure my backpack, which contained the classified shit, in my trunk, and to pay my priest a visit. I slid on my black leather gloves before pulling a black ski mask over my head. I checked both directions of the street and crossed the distance to my target.

The ground was covered with layers of delicate pink and white petals from the trees surrounding the perimeter, victims of the recent rain. If it hadn't been so warm, it could easily have been mistaken for snow. It wouldn't deter me if it was, because once I had my teeth in something, there was no stopping me. And the higher the stakes were, the more elaborate my plans became.

The darkness worked to my advantage, and many people weren't out due to the sudden changes in weather. What a difference a day made. The clear sky from yesterday was a stark difference from this damp and drizzly night. The evening cloaked my presence, allowing me to move somewhat freely. Since I had a dry run of breaking into Father Saint James's home yesterday, this would be a piece of cake.

I placed my hand above my forehead, away from the glass so I didn't leave a mark, and peeked through the window, searching for signs of the priest. Dancing shadows of the trees outside were the only movement inside. I crept along the back of the house, skimming the kitchen. Like the living room, there was no Father Saint James in sight. I tapped the screen of my watch to reveal the time. It was 9:45 p.m. Where could he be?

Wait—there, a faint light. I tiptoed, craning my neck to investigate the source. The office door was ajar, and the glow looked like that of a computer left on.

The window I used to enter the premises the first time was closed, forcing me to be creative. Thankful that I came prepared, I pulled two small metal rods out of my pocket and made my way to the back door. I crouched down, keeping an eye on the church—one could never be too cautious—pausing when chatter filled the air. Voices accompanied by skateboard wheels skidding across the ground floated from the street, loud then gradually soft again, and once they were gone, I went to town on the lock.

It only took one attempt. I slowly twisted the knob. The

door creaked, causing me to stop. If his lit computer was any indication, he had to be here somewhere. I waited for a few seconds and, when nobody came to check, I crept inside.

I sneaked into the living room via the kitchen hallway and, once again, stopped in my tracks as the sound of running water, coming from the main bedroom, caught my attention. I leaned against the wall, pressing my ears to the partition, before peeking in.

The bedroom was dim, steam issuing from the open ensuite. *That's where you are.* Lifting my boots quietly, I stepped heel to toe toward the bathroom in a feather-like manner.

Father Saint James hummed while he lathered his body with soap. It was easy to make out his shape through the mist, and the contours of his physique directed all my blood to my stirring cock. I released an inward groan when he twisted his body to rinse off, his ass pressing against the glass door. My mouth watered. I pulled the glove from my right hand and placed it in my back pocket. I snaked my hand under my belt and into my pants. Slick moisture covered my palm. I rubbed circles around the tip of my cock, spreading the pre-cum leaking out of the slit all over its head, falling into a lustful trance.

My senses were awakened when the running water stopped. I stepped back, looking around for a place to hide. I was just getting started and there was no way I was leaving now. Not until I was satisfied. The shower door slid open, followed by the sound of wet footsteps slapping on the tiles. I beelined to the closet, closing it from the inside.

Fuck. I groaned, enclosed with the scent of my newest obsession. The image of Father Saint James naked and glistening had my mind in a frenzy. I pulled my hand out of my pants because one more stroke and I would fucking bust a nut. Through the sliver of the closed closet door, I peeked through.

He was still in the bathroom, facing the mirror. Disappointment spread inside me—he was covered with a robe. My patience was being tested, and heaven knew it was short, almost non-existent.

I was rewarded when Father Saint James made his way out of the bathroom, the robe loosely wrapped around his waist. The lower part of his body was covered, but I couldn't miss the well-defined chest peering from within the thin shiny fabric. His pecs were glistening wet, making him even more alluring. He massaged the back of his neck, stretching it left and right, moaning as he applied pressure on his traps muscles where it met his shoulder. His Adam's apple protruded from his brawny neck, moving up and down as he swallowed. He released a deep breath before turning around.

Slowly, he loosened the fabric belt around his waist and disrobed, one arm at a time. My breath caught; it was a sight to behold. My speculation from the first time I saw him had been spot-on, at least where his ass was concerned. His butt cheeks were round and firm, melon size, with dimples on each. His back muscles flexed and relaxed, tapering down to a trimmed waist. Had I known about the show waiting for me, I would've brought my phone to capture one of the most seductive and erotic moments I'd ever seen—and I'd seen plenty.

I kneeled, unbuttoning my pants, then pulled my zipper one tooth at a time to prevent it from making noise. My boxers followed, stopping mid-thigh. The girth of my cock swelled, pre-cum dripping onto the wooden floor. I almost lost it when

Father Saint James turned to hang the robe on the hook next to the closet. I held my breath, my heart skipping a beat at the prospect of being caught in such a compromising position. Not having my gun—or any weapon—with me should've rang all sorts of warning bells. But based on my thorough investigation earlier, I knew the priest didn't have a weapon. Well, except what he was packing between his legs.

From this vantage point, Father Saint James was a vision. Who fucking knew priests could be this beefy: bulging biceps, chiseled sixpack, and obliques for days. My tongue would have a field day licking the soft happy trail leading to the promised land. *Fuck me, Jesus.* Father Saint James adjusted his dick and, in an instant, it reacted from his touch, nearly doubling in size, his equally impressive balls hanging below. Being the holy man he was, he stopped before his cock turned into a full-mast salute.

I was salivating, and if I didn't calm down, this would be over way too soon. I paced myself with long drawn-out strokes. He walked to the dresser near the window; my eyes followed his every move. He grabbed his phone and tapped it to life, its backlight illuminating his face. He swiped and tapped, before bringing the phone to his ear, presumably to check his voice mail. He frowned, his grip on his phone tightening. His lips drew into a line, agitation evident in his features. After a couple of minutes, he tossed the device on the top of the wooden dresser before walking toward his bed, where he relaxed on the comforter, staring at the ceiling, deep in thought.

My attention was divided between the specimen of a man lying on the bed naked and the phone sitting on his dresser. It buzzed, the accompanying light brightening the corner of the dim room. He ignored it, and I wondered why.

I shook my head and focused on the naked priest. *Come on, play with your cock*, I prayed, then realized just how fucked up that was. Here I was, praying for a priest to jack his meat while I jerked off in sync with his rhythm. That alone should be enough to stop me—but then again, it was me. Call me sick, but who wasn't these days?

Father Saint James closed his eyes, running his hand from his chest to his navel down to his semi-chub. He gripped his dick, stroking it until its head was swollen, angry, and red. The tip was slick. Two pumps later, he stopped. He opened his eyes, confusion written all over them. Glints of heat and guilt flashed alternately. My fascination for the priest grew watching him battle an internal war, but in the end the urge for pleasure won, as his left hand cupped and played with his balls while the other stroked his dick in a frenzy.

I matched his moves. My eyes trained on his face, watching his eyes roll into his head, his toes curling. His heavy breathing reverberated through the room, fighting with the sounds of slapping flesh.

I double-fisted my cock, my palms dragging from base to tip.

"Oh my …" Father Saint James muttered. His hips thrust into his balled hand, his leg muscles flexing as he moved up and down. The wooden headboard rapped the wall, rattling the hanging artwork. Inaudible words came out of his wide-open mouth. His whole body trembled until one last thrust. Thick white cum jetted out of his cock, pulse by pulse, lasting for thirty seconds. When I thought the waves of pleasure had run its course, his dick continued to eject semen, soaking his abs.

The carnal sounds, the vision of his euphoria, was a million times better than porn. I came so hard I saw spots. I jacked off until the last drop of cum dripped onto the floor. When my breathing steadied, I looked down at the mess I'd made and grabbed an item of clothing from the hamper to erase the evidence of my demented display.

Father Saint James hopped off the bed, hands on his stomach, preventing his wad from dripping onto the floor. He walked briskly to the bathroom and, when I heard him enter the shower and start the water, I waited a couple of seconds before coming out of the closet.

I stopped and glanced at his cell. What had upset him? "Damn it," I whispered when it asked for a passcode. The running water stopped and I was out of his room in seconds.

Back at my car, I found him looking out the window. It was hard to tell, but I could swear he was staring in my direction. I was certain he couldn't see me. It was dark and the pouring rain had started again. I waited for a minute and, when his light turned off, I pressed the ignition button and drove off.

There was a line where obsession ended and insanity began. I was not a betting man, but if I was, I'd wager I had just crossed that line ten times. *Does that make me crazy?*

Eleven: The Priest

Sunday came, which meant my first homily at the Cathedral of Holy Cross. It should be precisely like any other sermon I'd given, but this one carried a heavier weight. I checked my reflection in the mirror one last time before heading out of my bedroom, ignoring the open laptop and secured file mocking me from the office. My chance to make a good impression relied on this mass.

Last night, Jessica had asked for a preview, but aside from the scriptures and verses we were using for the mass, I'd given her nothing about the liturgy. The truth was, I hadn't made up my mind yet. The last couple of days had been a blur and I had yet to have a full night's sleep. Living on three to four hours of rest would soon catch up with me. Besides, my experience had given me a few available sermons to deploy. I would decide which one to use once I had the pulse of the assembly.

We were lined up by the door of the church for the entrance procession to commence the beginning of the mass when the man with no name walked by. His blazing gaze bored a hole in my already fragile self-control. He bumped into a couple of people as he made his way inside, giving them a death glare when they looked back at him. They were reduced to shaking their heads. This was church, after all, on Sunday no less. Unaffected by the disapproving glances, he made his way inside. I watched him enter a pew near the back, standing until one of the parishioners already seated acknowledged his presence. The parishioner didn't move. Mr. No Name scowled at the older man until he scooted toward the middle, giving him room. He must've been intimidated by the man in black as he conceded considerable space, enough for three people.

"Ready?" Jessica asked.

I returned my focus, took a deep breath, and nodded. "Yeah." *Here goes nothing.*

It went well. The final moments of the mass closed in and the congregation was yet to show any signs of approval or disdain for my presence. All eyes were on me. *Are they even paying attention?* I thought when I combed the standing-room-only crowd. I doubted they were. I wouldn't be surprised if they were waiting for a slip-up to fuel their narrative that I was too young to lead them. If there was one thing I'd learned these past few days from meeting parishioners, Father Oller was beloved by everyone. Here I was thinking the only big shoes I had to fill were those of my family.

The choir standing in front of the balcony housing the brass organ sang the final hymn of the mass. Everyone rose to their feet, joining the chorus. Jessica clapped her hands, looking around, beaming. Tim, the church courier, followed, urging more people to join until everyone accompanied them.

The explosion of applause was deafening. Finally, I could breathe.

Everyone was on their feet except for the man in the black hoodie, similar to what he was wearing when I met him during his confession. You couldn't miss the scar that slashed through his left eyebrow, dangerously close to his eye. An imperfection that could have easily been labeled a flaw, but somehow it made him appear remarkable. The angry puckered skin was a stunning feature, giving him an aura of fierceness. He was looking straight at me with an intensity that matched his strong square jaw and cheekbones. The chill in his gaze overwhelmed the warmth in his eyes.

"Father," the sacristan called. His soft voice and the hymn of the choir, ushering the congregation to the communion, brought my attention back to the mass.

The giant organ played louder, filling the church with calls of angels.

I glanced back in the man's direction, only to find the pew vacated. He was gone.

He'd be back. I saw it in his eyes.

Lines formed for the communion toward the center and both sides of the church. The throng of churchgoers heading to the middle to receive their communion from me was longer than to the ministers to my sides, handling and feeding the congregation with thin white wafers. Today had been a success judging by the applause and friendly smiles around.

"That was a great sermon, Father," an older lady said before opening her mouth to accept the body of Christ.

I nodded. "Thank you."

A dozen more of the same remarks followed, and for the first time in days, I could finally relax. The notion was short-lived as the Callahans made their way toward the front of the line, behind three other people. Their blank expressions gave nothing away. I held my breath when Mrs. Callahan stood before me. "The body of Christ," I said, placing the wafer on her opened palm.

"Amen," she said. She turned, only to stop before taking her first step. "That was great, Father Saint James. Very impressive," she huffed, the admission appearing to induce pain.

That was unexpected, but I'd take it. "Thank you. I'll see you around," I said.

The line shortened, the crowd thinned, until the church was empty—with the exception of the man in black standing at the back of the church. He had a steely and determined look, exuding an aura of intrigue.

I knew he'd be back, but I didn't anticipate it to be so soon. Either way, excitement coursed through me. It was something unfamiliar. I swallowed hard at the reminder of a few nights prior, when I'd let weakness take me over and had pleasured myself with the image of him.

"Everything is put away, Father," one of the sacristans said.

"Umm." I cleared my throat and glanced at the two young men. "Thank you both. Great job today."

"Is there anything else you need?" Jessica asked from behind me.

"No, but thank you," I answered, looking back at her. I was hoping they would leave soon.

She climbed the four-step altar, standing next to the two sacristans. Three sets of eyes were on me.

"You should go. I'll finish up here," I said.

"Are you sure?" she asked.

I nodded. "Go on. Enjoy this beautiful Sunday."

They exchanged glances until Jessica spoke. "As long as you're sure."

"I am. Thank you all for your help. I couldn't have asked

for a better first mass. Now, go." I motioned to the side doors, ushering them with a smile.

I directed my attention to the man in black after they left. He was planted in the same spot. I waited for him to move, to do something, until I'd had enough leering and gawking. He clearly needed something. Why would he stay otherwise?

The distance between us narrowed until I was standing in front of him. My heart was thumping, my palms sweating. I was equal parts nervous and excited to be this close to him. Hazel–green eyes studied me, a smirk appearing on his red lips. A few more scars were scattered on his face—his chin, his brows, his forehead—but nothing as prominent as the one over his left eye. You had to be near him to notice, and I doubted many had had the chance to be this close to him.

His eyes traveled to my lips.

I cleared my throat. "What's your name?"

"I told you. I'm nobody." He dragged his tongue to moisten his lips.

I was drawn, like a moth to a flame.

"What should I call you then?" What was up with all the games?

He raked my body from head to toe. "You can call me whatever you want, whenever you want."

I took a deep breath; my patience was being tested by his presence. I stepped forward, but the man wedged himself between me and the ajar door. Close enough that our faces were almost touching. His fresh breath fanned my lips, causing goosebumps all over my body. Thankful that I had my full regalia to hide his effect on me, I stood my ground. It wasn't the first time I'd found a man attractive, desirable, but it had been a long time since I'd acted on my temptations. That was when I was younger, before I was a priest. There wasn't room for temptations now. Men like me were destined to be alone, deprived of any affection, passion, and desire. I had one mission. To fulfill my commitment.

"Do you mind?" I asked. My voice was even, unaffected. If only he knew what was brewing inside me.

The man remained planted. He didn't move a single muscle, but somehow his silence and stare pulled desire from me, an emotion that should've been suppressed the moment I made my vow of devotion. His gaze intensified with undeniable lust. The scar on his left eye made him appear dangerous, out of reach. Irresistible.

The urge to run my finger along the crease of his eye came out of nowhere. "I have to go," I said, looking at my feet to avoid being lost in his eyes. I needed to get a grip, to get my senses under control.

"Then go," he said. His voice was huskier this time. "No one is stopping you … Father."

"Please." I didn't know what the plea was for, and I didn't have the time nor the energy to figure it out.

His head leaned closer to my ear. "Say that again," he whispered.

His warm, moist breath made me shiver, my knees weakening. "Please," I repeated.

He took a deep breath. "Fuuuuck," he moaned, exhaling. He lifted his hand, which also had a four-inch scar running from his wrist to his knuckles. I wanted to ask where he got them from, but I had a decent suspicion where. Time moved in slow motion. My senses were hyper-aware of his voice, his scent, his actions. His palm closed in on my face; our eyes locked; chests heaved. One more second and he would be touching

ELEVEN: THE PRIEST

me—and I was about to let him.

The door to the side of the church opened, the creaking hinges announcing someone's arrival. *Saved by the bell.* Surprised that neither of us jolted from the intrusion, I staggered back, expecting he'd do the same now that the moment had passed.

He didn't. Instead, he moved a step closer while glancing at the group of people entering the church, who were too busy admiring the palatial dome and hanging chandelier to pay attention to the sins unfolding feet away from them. Their smartphones attached to their selfie sticks would've captured us had they not been oblivious to our presence. He leaned in, dragging his neatly trimmed beard across my cheek until his mouth neared my ear—the one away from the unsuspecting crowd. "I can keep a secret," he whispered, the tip of his tongue licking my lobe. "It'll be our dirty little one, Father." A low chuckle escaped his mouth before he walked away.

A loud cackle from the group sobered me, allowing me to recalibrate back to equilibrium. That could never happen again. I would not jeopardize my mission for an impulse.

"Hi, Father," someone said when they finally noticed my presence.

I acknowledged them with a nod before heading toward one of the doors in the east wing of the church.

"Wait up," one of the guys said. "Can we take some pictures with you?"

Wanting to make a great first impression, I stopped walking to face them. "Sure," I said, smiling. These guys could be tourists for all I knew, highly likely judging by their Canucks NHL jerseys, who happened to beat Boston's Bruins last night. Still, I obliged. "I'd be happy to," I added, marching in their direction.

It'll be our dirty little secret, Father.

Twelve: The Reaper

I'd never been so bored in my entire fucking life. After what seemed like ten lifetimes, I was eager to get the hell out of this place where anything resembling fun came to die. It took a little over two hours to finalize the new lease for an apartment I didn't need, but after going through the bullshit of signing the contract and wiring funds for the deposit, I was out of the office before the ink was even dry. Figuratively.

"Mr. Smith," the property manager called.

I forgot her name. Maybe it was Jane or Jennifer. She looked like a Jennifer. I didn't bother learning it, since all I cared about was finding an apartment facing the bishop's house. Five units and three floors later, I was being ushered inside an apartment parallel to Father Saint James's bedroom window. The manager discussed terms and prices, but I was already tuned out, my mind spotting a location for my high-grade camera. She could have gouged the price of this unit tenfold and I wouldn't have cared, not for what it was worth to me.

"John!" she yelled when I ignored her first call. Maybe her name was Julia. What-fucking-ever. It didn't make a difference.

John Smith was one of the aliases I used to conceal my

identity. It was common enough, perhaps the most common name for a white guy. We didn't want our names to be remarkable, we wanted the opposite. The more we could get lost in the shuffle of common names, the better.

"Mr. John Smith," she repeated when I still didn't answer. I kept walking away.

Even through her exasperation, she couldn't hide the amusement in saying my name out loud. Fact: John Smith was a common name, but I had yet to meet someone with that name. I stopped, turning to face her. Her red heels clicked across the brick courtyard. I shrugged then crossed my arms when she reached me. *Emily*, her name tag said. My guesses were way off. Good thing I wasn't on an assignment.

"Did you hear me calling you?" she asked, her nostrils flaring. She was feisty for such a petite woman. She looked like one of the strippers I'd banged before. I preferred men, but sex was sex. Plus, you could always put a pillow over their faces. All they needed to have was a wet hole and you could color me pink.

"Did you see me walking away?" I answered her question with a question of my own. I'd had enough interactions with people and I'd spoken more today than I had all week.

Her mouth fell open. *Jerk*, she mouthed, but she may as well have said it out loud. "I was just gonna tell you that my boss said you can move in today," she said. "Here are your keys."

"K." I grabbed them from her hand, turned my back, and walked away. I was going to move in today with or without their approval. I didn't need keys, and I was only moving a few things with me.

She huffed and puffed. "What an ass."

Tell me something I don't know.

TWELVE: THE REAPER

***

After loading the laptop into my backpack, I unpacked my night goggles and the Canon 5D Mark IV buried deep within the metal chest I kept for mission-related paraphernalia. I grabbed the case that held the toolset on my way out of my bedroom. My cell phone buzzed in my pocket. *Unknown*, the caller ID flashed.

"Who the fuck is this?" I answered. Nothing but static noise filled the silence. I pressed my cell tighter to my ear, hoping to decipher the faint audio on the other line. My frustration grew. I ended the call, but my mind stalled. Very few people knew my number and I only used my cell for one purpose: to take calls from El Jefe for my new assignment. It wouldn't be The Savior because he only texted.

My phone vibrated again. *Unknown*, again. I answered right away. "Who. The fuck. Is this?" I spat. Voiceless static, again. My grip on the phone tightened; I fought the urge to throw it on the floor. In the end, I turned off the device and tossed it in my bag.

I grabbed my motorcycle keys and headed back to my new hideout to focus on the priest, instead of the anxiety brewing inside me. Father Saint James would be my distraction until whatever pull he had on me passed. I'd been here before, and once the novelty and thrill went away, I was off to the next shiny new thing. My fixation with Father Saint James would be no different. I didn't know if he was into anything—he was a man of God, after all—but one thing I knew for certain: my dick would be in him, and he would love every second of it.

I was hyper-vigilant cruising the city, especially after those two suspicious calls, even going as far as taking a different route. But aside from the occasional middle-finger salutes I received from those who couldn't drive as well as me, everything appeared as normal. I parked my bike in the uneven brick alley behind the apartment, ignoring the sour odor coming from two giant garbage bins. I headed inside the complex using the back door, opting to use the stairs since the elevator was one snap away from falling apart. "Hi," a random guy who was picking up his mail from the corner of the lobby said. I ignored him and jogged up the steps.

It took some jamming before the key slid into the hole, another reminder of how old this complex was. The door screeched, dragging on the wooden floor that was covered in marks outlining the opening and closing of it. It was a shithole. It made Motel 6 look like the fucking Four Seasons. The setting should've messed with my neatness compulsion, but the wreckage and chaos only heightened the stakes, making the prize of being inside Father Saint James much more satisfying. On cue, my dick perked up, urging me to hurry the fuck up and get on with it.

I kicked the door closed behind me; it locked as it hit the jam. I slid the white vertical plastic blinds up—left by the previous owner, according to Emily—until there was a six-inch gap from the frame, enough space for my lens. I retrieved my camera and pointed the lens at Father Saint James's bedroom window while adjusting the focus manually.

"Perfect," I said when I could read the time on the clock on the priest's nightstand. I attached the USB to my laptop so I had a bigger screen to observe his every move. "Fucking perfect."

The clarity of the video appeared as if someone was filming *in* his room. Satisfied with my setup and feeling somewhat accomplished, I headed out to pay someone a visit. Someone I'd been looking forward to seeing all year—not even Father Saint James could stop me doing that.

***

The golden color of dusk that bathed everything within its reach needed a special name. Thinking about the very limited memories I had from when I was younger, I closed my eyes, remembering a rich and vibrant laugh with strong arms around me. I rarely allowed myself to experience emotions. Feelings made us weak, clouding our judgment. But for now, I would succumb while I camped between two giant pine trees.

After hours of watching the familiar house next to a sugar maple tree, I carefully surveyed my surroundings. The wooden swing we built, hanging from one of the maple's sturdy branches, still remained. I watched every vehicle and individual passing through my night goggles, making sure no one managed to trail me without my knowledge. Being here was dangerous, but this was the last shred of myself I wasn't willing to give up. Yet. The two-hundred-and-twenty-mile annual trek to this quiet town was something I looked forward to. But as much as it wrecked me to admit, this would be the last time. A lot of things had changed over the past few months and it was only a matter of time before those who were after me succeeded. I would be ready when that day came.

Belfast, Maine, hadn't changed. Residents of this town must not have heard of streetlights, since it was almost pitch-black out so early in the evening. The sleepy coastal community used to be my home. I stepped from my hiding spot before I fell into a rabbit hole of memories that would take me days to unravel. Another reason why I shouldn't be here. Memories of this town exposed the chinks in my armor, and I needed my shield to be stronger than ever.

I dropped a bouquet of yellow roses and a box wrapped in silver and gold paper on the porch before jogging back to my hiding spot, to wait for signs of movement from the house. My attention traveled back to the old swing and I wondered when someone had last used it.

"Higher!" The voice of the young me echoed in my head. I remembered that carefree kid. He was fun. Loved.

I envied him.

A couple of hours had gone by and still nothing. I stayed put because I knew they were inside. The lights in the Victorian home were on. There was no way they would forget. I had visited on this day every year for the last twelve years, and the mere thought that they had forgotten me made my chest hurt. Even if they had no idea it was me.

My breath hitched when the porch light came to life. I lowered my goggles to see closely and clearly in the dark. I held my breath when the door opened. A couple in their late seventies appeared, slowly making their way outside. My heart squeezed at the sight of the woman using her cane. They were a lot older now, the past decade having taken a toll on them. The older man bent over, slowly, as if he was moving in slow motion, grimacing along the way. He picked up the flowers and gifts, handing the present to his lovely wife.

The older woman beamed and looked around. But, as always, their smiles faltered when they realized the mysterious giver would never be revealed. She wrapped her arms around her husband, resting her head on his chest. They were so beautiful together. That was what love looked like.

I raised my goggles so I could read their lips. *"Just like the last one,"* the man said.

"They're gorgeous. I wish I knew who left them." She looked up and met his eyes.

He didn't respond. Instead, he kissed the top of her head. They searched the dark one last time, their gaze skimming past me several times, before going back inside.

"Happy birthday, Grandma." I fought the urge to go after them and hug them. I wanted to tell them that the grandson they mourned was still alive, but I couldn't risk the lives of the only people I truly cared for. My eyes stung, blinking tears away before they fell. "I love you both."

Hours later, I was wide awake. The visit to my grandparents had ripped open old wounds. I decided it would be the last time I would ever see them. I was playing with fire, and as much as it pained me to cut the last cord attaching me to my old life, I couldn't be selfish anymore. It was becoming dangerous for them, and I couldn't bear the thought of someone hurting my grandparents to get to me.

Thirteen: The Priest

Butterflies filled my stomach at the prospect of encountering the unnamed man again. It had been days since I'd seen him last. Four days, to be exact, but who was counting. I wasn't going to admit it, but during the confession hours I had hoped to see him, for a couple of reasons: To thank him for saving me from being mugged, and to satisfy my curiosity about him. He was a peculiar man and I wanted to know what made him who he was. Reading people and their behavior was something I'd mastered from the ministry. The ability to extract a deeper meaning enabled me to discover information about them even if they weren't willing to share, and the only way to get to his secrets was to spend time with him. I was certain he'd be back. Guilt and confession were a mental cycle, and once you were trapped, escape was impossible. Confessing one's sins was a cyclical Band-Aid, a tool to help one heal without the long therapy sessions.

I began to pray to purge the mysterious man from my thoughts. Sitting in the confessional waiting for the next person could get mind-numbing.

The curtain on the other side of the booth was yanked open

THIRTEEN: THE PRIEST

with impatience. My lips pulled into a smile; I knew who my confessor was without looking into the partition. The manner at which he sat himself with a flump to announce his arrival before angrily pulling the curtain closed made my heart flip. My speculation was confirmed when our eyes connected. The unnamed man crossed his arms. His black sweatshirt was like a second skin and couldn't hide his bulky arms, stacked with muscles. He smelled like citrus and mint, a vice I hoped to never begin. "Tell me your name," I said, trying my luck one more time.

"Not gonna happen," he said. The man shifted in his seat and my eyes traveled down to his thick thighs. I swallowed hard.

"Why not?" I didn't know why I was pushing it so hard, but my curiosity about him had reached a level beyond comprehension. "It's just a name," I added.

"I don't wanna have to kill you," he answered. The intensity in his eyes burned. "Besides, I told you, you can call me anything … any time." A sinister smile crossed his red lips, exposing his perfect set of teeth.

"You wouldn't," I said. "But I'm not afraid of dying," I admitted. The statement was true. Everyone had a shelf life, and the bliss that came with understanding we would perish at some point freed me from the guilt.

He didn't respond. It seemed that I'd caught him off guard. We let the uncomfortable silence linger between us; I was hoping he would be the first to budge. He wasn't. "I haven't thanked you for saving me from those guys," I said, breaking the deafening silence.

"They haven't bothered you, have they?" His jaw tightened and he balled his hands into meaty fists. "Did they come here?"

A storm brewed in his eyes. This man had a short fuse. "Are you okay?"

"No." I shook my head. "I mean, I'm okay, and no, they haven't bothered me. They don't know I'm the bishop." Even if they did know, I doubt they'd remember. Those men were trashed.

"Good. Because I'd kill them."

"There's no need for that. I could've handled it myself," I said.

"Yeah right." He chuckled. "They could've seriously hurt you. Plus, what were you planning to do? Pray their sins away?" he mocked.

"Do you always resort to killing?" I asked, ignoring the annoyance caused by his assumption that I couldn't take care of myself.

"Only for the right people. Or, should I say, the wrong people."

"Why aren't you in jail?" That question kept me up at night. Well, *him* and that question.

"Because I'm good at my job," he answered. "Fuck," he whispered, looking away.

"Killing is your job?" As expected, he didn't answer. But unlike the last time, he stayed. "What were you doing when you helped me that early in the morning, by the way?"

He answered with a shrug.

"This is where you're supposed to flee, like last time," I said, reminding him of our first meeting. It was a risky move but it paid off when he remained in his seat.

"What do you fucking want?" he asked. His lips were tight, eyes burning. His body language screamed agitation.

"I don't need anything," I lied. "You seek *me* in this place of worship." He would need to try harder if he wanted to intimidate me. This was my territory.

"You're different from all the priests I've met before," he said, eyeing me.

"Different how? Because I care enough to ask questions?"

As predictable as Sundays falling after Saturdays, he met my question with a shrug followed by another wave of silence.

Why is he still here? I thought. *Why do I want him to stay?* Subtly, I took deep breaths and changed the course of our conversation. "Are you here for another confession?" I'd never asked anyone that question before. We were trained to never ask. *It makes people feel judged.* The man was like any other, and I wanted our conversation to keep going so I could gain his trust. "You were just here a week ago."

He leaned back in his seat. "Church is open to everyone the last time I checked," he said, smirking. He must've been waiting for the shift in our exchange judging by the twinkle in his eyes. "Have you thought about my offer?" He stared at my face, then my lips. He spread his muscular thighs apart, revealing a bulging crotch.

My gaze traveled down to his groin, and I was rendered unable to speak because my mouth suddenly dried up.

"See something you like?" He pulled the zipper of his pants, slowly dragging it down. He moistened his lips with his tongue. "All you gotta do is ask," he whispered in a magnetic hum.

The zipper was halfway down. I should stop this. This was a church in the middle of the day. Anyone could walk in. Still, I let him proceed until it was all the way down.

His eyes were yet to leave my face. He paused, perhaps to gauge my reaction. He pulled a gun from his waistband, laying it next to him. That alone should've sounded the alarm in my head, but I'd seen guns before and knew my way around them. I held my breath as he unbuttoned the top, revealing black underwear with a white waistband. The length of his dick was outlined perfectly. He lowered them, exposing a trail of fine blond hair leading to a girthy cock. He lifted his sweatshirt, revealing ridges of smooth, lean abs. "Do you like this, Father?"

I groaned. My mind was in a haze. I shook my head and cleared my throat. "What are you doing?" I asked, my voice an octave higher than usual.

"Do you want me to stop?" he asked, pulling his underwear even lower. His obliques were out of this world. Defined and veiny.

God, make it stop, I told myself, but I couldn't seem to get the words out of my mouth.

"It'll be our dirty little secret," he repeated.

The church's door creaked open, carrying a conversation inside. I expected the man to stop his display. But, to my surprise, he appeared more excited. Mischief in his eyes matched the sinister smile on his lips. He stroked the length of his dick through the fabric, the shape of its head visible, the pre-cum darkening the soft cotton.

The chatter became distinctive, the footsteps louder. The newcomers were mere feet away.

I summoned what was left of my self-control before someone opened a curtain and found us. "Stop." It was supposed to be an order, but it sounded like a plea. "Stop," I repeated with authority.

"What was that?" a voice outside asked.

"I think it's coming from the booth," the other voice answered. "Are you okay over there?"

"Yes," I answered.

The man in front of me chuckled before standing, pulling his zipper up and buttoning his pants. "I'll be back tonight," he whispered, tucking the gun into his waistband.

"The church will be locked," I said, when I should've said *Don't come back.*

A laugh escaped his mouth as he grabbed the curtain. I had a feeling locked doors wouldn't stop him. It didn't matter. I wouldn't be here. I shouldn't be here.

"Archer," he whispered.

"Huh?" I asked. I was so shocked my brain misfired.

"My name is Archer," he repeated before yanking the curtain back so hard it startled an "Oh!" out of one of the people standing nearby.

What a fitting name for someone like him.

"Archer," I whispered.

Fourteen: The Reaper

I didn't know what possessed me to tell Father Saint James my real name. I could've easily pulled a fake name out of my ass. But, like the last time we were together in the confinement of his confession booth, I was all out of sorts because of him. His face was painted with shock, and I had to repeat my name a second time before he realized what I'd said. My brain knew what needed to be done, but my mouth seemed to have a mind of its own. The truth was, I wanted to hear how my name sounded coming from his lips. I didn't get a chance to find out since I marched out of there before he ever said it.

Before I was The Reaper, I'd had another name. The one that was passed through four generations, starting with my great-grandfather down to me, where it would end. It was a kind name. It was a name no one feared. Archer Dawson. I loved that name. But, just like my former life, it had to be buried six feet in the ground. Because, to the rest of the world, I no longer existed.

My friends used to call me Archie. My grandparents called me Little Arch, not to be mistaken for Big Arch—my father—and Grand Arch, belonging to my grandpa. My

FOURTEEN: THE REAPER

recollection of my parents was murky. Sometimes, I got bits and pieces of them through vague memories and vivid dreams. But I questioned how many of them were true or were a product of my imagination and wishful thinking. I didn't know much about my mom and dad, but my grandparents I remembered very well, even though I wish I didn't.

My father was killed in the Gulf War, or at least that was what my mom told me before disappearing herself ten days after my father's death, forcing my grandparents to look after me at eight years old. Vividly, I could still remember that night when they came for me, one of the very few fragments of my childhood etched into my head.

It was during the dead of winter. It had snowed the night before and a white blanket covered the ground. The door flew open, frigid air invading the dark house. I had run out of newspapers and books to burn after two days. I was too hungry and weak to gather wood outside during the storm. The house was so cold.

Dark silhouettes appeared. "Archer!" my grandpa yelled. It should've been the first sign of the horror that would come after. He never called me by that name unless I was in trouble or something serious was about to happen. I didn't know it then, but it would be the beginning of the series of unfortunate events coming my way. My grandparents tried to shield me from it, but they could only do so much where The Firm was concerned. My grandparents were David to The Firm's Goliath. Only in this story, David didn't win.

The cold winter breeze gushed through the wide-open door, carrying flakes of snow inside. I opened my mouth to say something but my body was numb, perhaps from sitting under the table for two days straight. "In here," I croaked.

"Archer, my love, where are you?" my grandma repeated when she didn't hear me. She closed the door and flipped the light switch,

to no avail—the power had been out for a couple of days; no heat either.

I swallowed my spit to clear my throat, grimacing from the pain. It was as if tiny pins and needles were piercing my windpipes. "In here," I yelled, hoping they could locate me with my weakened voice. I'd moved under the table two days ago after the men who ransacked our house had left. They barged in when I was in my bedroom waiting for my mother.

"You will be safe here," my mom used to tell me as she was building a small compartment under the floor of my closet. "Remember, when I tell you to hide, this is where I need you to go, okay?" She must've said those words a few times, and when I was finally older she told me: "There are some bad guys out there and they might look for us."

So, when the door opened with a loud bang and noise from the chaos downstairs carried to my room, I hid. Hungry and afraid, I emerged after a couple of days. Our house had been turned upside down. Papers were scattered everywhere, and a mound of snow was blocking the still-open door. I used my legs and pushed the door with my back, shoving the snow outside. I was in the middle of inspecting the damage when lightning struck one of the poles outside, killing the lights. Out of fear, I ran under the only piece of furniture left standing: the dining table.

"I'm here, Grandma," I called with what was left of my energy.

"Oh, my baby," she said, rushing to me. She pressed her warm hands on my cold cheeks. "My goodness, you're frozen." Her voice was laced with relief and concern, tears cascaded down her cheeks.

Grandpa removed his jacket and wrapped it around my frail body.

That was all I could remember from that evening. It was funny how memories worked. Sometimes, no matter how

FOURTEEN: THE REAPER

hard you tried to remember more, the mind wouldn't let you.

I sucked in a lungful of fresh air and, once sobered from my body's response to Father Saint James, I realized that revealing my name should be the least of my concerns, especially after admitting that I killed for a living. "Fuck!" I cursed, punching my helmet out of frustration. This had to stop before it turned into something I couldn't control. I had to end it tonight.

I climbed onto my bike, turning the ignition on. My phone vibrated; the watch synced to my cell notified me of an incoming call from a New York City area code. Ignoring the call, I whipped out of Boston to go to my 'office,' the makeshift building made from an old shipping container. My phone buzzed again. The tiny watch screen displayed the same number. After half a dozen persistent calls, I pulled over. "What?" I barked into the phone.

"This is Marilyn. Can you talk?" Marilyn Ellis was a fearless investigative journalist, covering the most dangerous stories, from the cartel to bombings in the Middle East. She'd made a name for herself by exposing corruption, fraud, and the wrongdoings of companies and politicians. She took no prisoners when it came to finding the truth. "Are you there?" she asked after I didn't answer.

"Yeah, I can talk."

"Give me the list and I'll expose them," she said.

Shocked, I asked, "What made you change your mind?" Marilyn had initially said no when I'd reached out to her months ago. I didn't blame her. If I didn't live in the shadows, I would've called myself insane.

"Long story," she said.

"Interesting," I replied. There was a long silence and I thought I'd lost her.

Muffled footsteps filled my ear followed by the sound of a door shutting. "Sorry. I had to find a safe place to talk," she whispered. "Crazy things have been happening since we met and I'm starting to think you're right."

"I don't have the list yet, but I will get it. I just need more time," I said. I wished I had more time.

"Okay," Marilyn whispered. "But whatever you do, be careful."

"Where are you?" I asked. She was one of my last hopes. I couldn't afford to lose another person. It'd been a few days since I'd heard from Tobias and he hadn't responded to any of my calls. I sure hoped nothing had happened to him. William's death was awful, and it also meant one less person to fight this war with me.

"I'm at the studio. I'm about to head home," she said through the clinking of keys.

"Are you safe?"

"In my line of work?" She scoffed. "Get that list. The sooner you get it, the sooner we can expose them. I have to go." The call ended and I was left staring at my phone.

I needed to get that list from The Firm and I couldn't afford to attract suspicion about what I was doing. Not until the proof was in my possession. "One more assignment," I said, putting my helmet back on, glancing behind for traffic before merging onto the road. I needed to get to the storage container and devise a way to obtain that list.

I was in the middle of skimming through hundreds of files I'd downloaded onto my laptop when El Jefe's name flashed on my screen. "Damn it!" I cursed. I cleared my throat before answering the call. "What?"

El Jefe chuckled. "Hello to you too," he greeted. "Where are you?"

"Jacking off," I answered. Irritation coursed through me. Why did it matter where I was? "What do you need?"

He sighed. He was used to my abruptness. "I'm calling about your assignment. You leave for Monaco tomorrow. Same routine." He hung up.

Fuck. I was hoping I had more time. I had loads of things to do and very little time to accomplish them. It didn't help that my attention was divided between The Firm, my assignment, and Father Saint James. I slammed the computer shut and checked my backpack for the documents from my last visit with El Jefe.

The folder contained a United States passport with my picture and a completely different name: *Peter Robinson.* Another generic name that was okay by me. A stash of Euro bills was bound together with a rubber band. The last item was a photograph of a creepy man with sunken, beady eyes and tar-stained teeth. He had a bony face riddled with pockmarks. I flipped the photo over and read his name: *Max Lancaster.* Below his name was a laundry list of shitty deals he'd done, but nothing more glaring than trafficking women, forcing them to record themselves in compromising situations while Max performed degrading acts on them. He was the self-appointed king of the dark web.

"Not for long, fucker. I'm gonna have fun with you," I muttered.

I packed everything into my bag before grabbing my phone to send another text to Tobias. I fucking hoped he was all right. I stared at the small screen, thinking about what to say. I didn't want to sound like I cared, even though I did. Tobias was a great man. I trusted him and I knew he trusted me—why else was he willing to put his life on the line to help me? If circumstances were different, we could've been friends, but, like what El Jefe said, everyone who had the misfortune of getting close to my sorry ass ended up dead.

I typed *Hey man, hope ur ok* but deleted it. *What's up man?* I cringed after reading that, touching the delete button aggressively until the message was blank. "It shouldn't be this fucking hard," I groaned, looking at the empty walls in my office. Minutes later, I decided to be honest and sent Tobias the message he deserved. He'd done so much for me and I owed him the truth. *I haven't heard from you. I'm starting to worry. Call me.*

Grabbing my keys, I headed out. But instead of heading home, I rode my motorcycle back to my shitty new apartment, because nothing said running out of time like spending it creeping on a priest.

Because it was me, and the only way I knew how to deal with any type of stress was sex, I headed to the window where my camera and laptop were located as soon as I arrived. I played the video recording of my personal Jesus, at triple speed to save time, starting from the time I left the church. Fucking boring! Nothing but windows and what appeared to be church staff passing by Father Saint James's brick home.

"Where the hell are you?" I switched from the screen to the camera, zooming out to scout his perimeter for any signs of him. I glanced at my watch to check the time. It was almost eight. The urge to see the priest burrowed into my already fucked-up mind. And because two of my personalities were kill mode and horny, I fished a condom and lube from my backpack before heading out. My dick twitched at the possibility of him waiting in the church for me. I had told him

FOURTEEN: THE REAPER

I would be back tonight, after all.

As expected, the main church door was locked. I walked to the west wing, where a smaller version of the same ornate wooden door was located, looking around to make sure no one was there. With the darkness of night and my black outfit, it would be hard for anyone to spot me. I kneeled, sliding my lock-picking tools into the keyhole. The lock clicked.

You could hear a pin drop with how quiet the church was at night. The main chandelier hanging in the middle of the altar was off, and the only light came from a couple of dim recessed wall sconces and wasn't enough to see everything inside. But there was one particular soft glow that caught my attention. I grinned. I had him hook, line, and fucking sinker.

With one goal in mind, I let my feet take me to the confessional, where I knew Father Saint James was waiting for my sins.

Fifteen: The Priest

od help me.

G   I wanted to forget why I was sitting in the booth staring through the screen at the empty seat in front of me. My hands were joined, resting on my lap, as I replayed all the reasons why I should walk away. Repercussions of succumbing to my weakness flashed in my mind, but still I remained seated. The door from the west wing scraped the floor. It was faint, but there was definitely movement out there. I closed my eyes, listening to the sound of soft footsteps approaching. I leaned back, my heart thumping. Excitement, fear, and lust concocted a recipe for a perfect disaster stronger than reason. The steps grew heavier, louder. The curtain opened and so did my eyes.

Archer stepped in wearing a black jacket, a black shirt, and black jeans. He sat on the cushioned bench and leaned back, his eyes glued to mine as he slowly closed the curtain. He suddenly leaned forward, sliding the partition open. "I knew you'd be here," he said. His sultry voice was captivating; I was under his spell.

I cleared my throat. "What has brought you here?"

The cavernous church was quiet. There was a stillness.

FIFTEEN: THE PRIEST

Perhaps the calm before the storm. Jessica had long ago gone home and there wasn't the usual contingent of people needing my attention. We were truly alone in this small box, an island in a vast sea of religion.

As a man of the cloth and a vessel for God, I had already breached several layers of protocol, but I'd lost all sense of right or wrong. My oath of celibacy had already been tarnished, and here I sat, a small barrier between me and a man I secretly craved. I wanted him to use my pious body. To take control.

Archer stood. "What brought me here?" he parroted. "That's almost humorous, Father."

He removed his leather jacket, revealing another layer of black; a garment in the guise of a T-shirt that was stretched to bursting by muscle. His chest was tight and defined, sexy nipples poking through the thin cloth. After laying his jacket in the corner of his tiny space, he slowly removed the shirt.

I considered myself to be a steady person. Patience and a calm demeanor were my trademarks. Archer, however, had me stiffening with anticipation of what he might do next. Faint scars peppered his chest and arm; a larger one with stitch placement still visible ran along his left oblique. Defined abdominals lined his midsection like a roadmap to my new hell. Everything pointed down to his low-riding black denim.

"Stop," I whispered.

"Do you want me to stop?" he asked, playing with the metal button above the zipper of his jeans.

"I ... don't," I panted.

"You don't what, Father?"

My pulse thumped in my ears. "I don't want you to stop."

Archer grinned, looking down at his bulging crotch. He

undid the button of his pants, then unzipped them. With a gentle tug, the jeans fell from his hips to his ankles. He wasn't wearing underwear.

"What do we have here, Father?" he teased, cupping his balls and lifting them up.

"This is a mistake," I said, panic coursing through my body. One problem: My excitement was beginning to overpower any common sense I had left. Archer stood naked, stroking his cock, while I remained seated on my side of the booth. His biceps seemed flexed even when they were relaxed, particularly the one attached to the hand jerking his dick. I studied him with adulation. He was an amazing specimen of man; a vision. His wide chest and broad shoulders tapered down to a slim waist. His thighs were thick and cut, supporting the splendor above them. As blasphemous as it was, he was a god.

"Why don't you spend less time worrying about your holier-than-thou crap and get over here and suck my cock?" he ordered.

"I can't."

"The fuck you can't," he hissed. "Now, do as I say, Father, and strip that pretty little dress of yours off."

"It's a cassock, not a dress."

"I don't care if it's Cinderella's ball gown. Dump it on the floor and get your sweet ass over here."

The way Archer spoke was hypnotizing. On one hand, he was crude and offensive. On the other hand, it drove me mad with desire. I'd always wondered about being dominated and I now wanted to be owned by him. I was always in control of every facet of my life, it'd be nice to be told what to do for once.

FIFTEEN: THE PRIEST

I knew walking away was the right thing to do, but deep down inside, where I kept my demons suppressed, was a passion burning so strong I was willing to cast aside all decorum and sensibilities for a taste of what he offered. Oh, I wanted him.

I unbuttoned the cassock, starting from the top, letting it fall behind me, and then stood in a white shirt and boxers.

"All of it," he insisted. His voice was firm as he commanded my every move.

I lacked the power to say no at this point, so I did as I was told. Once naked, we both were motionless and I waited for further instructions. None came, making me shiver from anticipation and the chilliness of the air.

"Well?" I asked.

"Stand still, Father. I'll tell you what's next." He raked my body with lust, grinning as his eyes fixated on my erection. "And you act like you don't want this." A humorless laugh escaped his mouth. "Your cock speaks otherwise."

Archer sat down on the bench and spread his legs wider. His balls were exposed under his stiff erection, which was leaning slightly as it tried to hold its girth upright. He brought his hands to his ripped stomach and dragged them over it, occasionally brushing across the tip of his dick.

"I can't do this," I said. "Not here."

"Come to me, Father. Now."

He was steel and I was a magnet. There was no ignoring his command.

I stepped from the booth and into the vast darkness of my church, glancing toward the crucifix. *Forgive me.*

I stood in front of his half of the booth, giving myself one more chance to walk away. I should've walked—ran, even—from what waited on the other side.

But, like all sinners, I was weak.

I pulled the curtain open.

"On your knees, Father. For once, I want you on your knees, instead of you demanding we bow to you. Not tonight. Not tonight."

I fell to my knees and had his swollen cock in my mouth instantly. My original plan was to torment him by teasing up and down his shaft with my warm and wet mouth, but he made it abundantly clear he had other plans. He held the back of my head and forced me onto his cock. I gagged and spit air as I tried to pull away but he was too strong and showed no signs of relinquishing control. I felt the first tinge of fear spread across my skin. I was in a small space with a murderer. All the signs were there. I'd made a huge mistake. And yet, I was thrilled beyond any euphoria I'd experienced.

Archer used his free hand to yank my hair. I might be a priest but this wasn't my first experience. I became comfortable with being face-fucked and reached for his balls, squeezing and tugging on them aggressively. He squirmed in his seat as the pain and pleasure shot through him. Two people could play this game.

"What's this, Father?" he asked. "I knew you were a cocksucker the moment I laid eyes on your pretty face. I hope you have more in you than that pathetic attempt at foreplay."

I pulled his balls harder as his body stiffened, instantly extending his legs straight out, nearly knocking me over.

My hands slid over his stomach on the way to his nipples. Once there, I secured each one between my thumbs and index fingers, gently teasing and twisting, nothing too crazy yet. His cock twitched in my throat so I knew I had his attention.

FIFTEEN: THE PRIEST

He moaned and stiffened, his body so rigid he was nearly horizontal in the booth. I waited like a cheetah crouching low in the grass, allowing him to relax and walk blindly into my trap.

"Fuck yeah," he moaned, removing his hand from the back of my head and grabbing a wrist for more control in case I decided to get rough.

Once free from being gagged by his girth, I gently tugged my hand free so I could slide up and down his length, twisting and slobbering all over him. He relaxed in pleasure and let me take more control of his cock. I continued sucking him, taking him deep and then pulling off him, massaging his balls until I was sure he was calm.

Relaxing my jaw, I took him in deep, my hands finding his sensitive nipples again. It was then I wrenched his nipples and wouldn't let go when he struggled under a strength he hadn't known I possessed. He tried to wriggle away but his cock was still in my mouth and he must've been afraid of what I might do to it if he struggled too much.

I came off his dick, moved one hand to his balls and secured them in a tight grip. His nuts looked like a water balloon as I squeezed. My other hand clamped a nipple tightly and then I twisted it as hard as I could.

"You want rough?" I spat. "I can give you rough."

"That's all you got?" he asked. "What the fuck is this, Sunday school?"

I moved my face to the inside of his thigh. He probably assumed I went there for some more oral teasing, but he'd be wrong. I bit down on a tendon in his groin and twisted his nipple again, causing him to yank my hair. He held me away from him by the hair and glared at me. Maybe he did have limits. But then he grinned and his eyes sparkled with insane delight. Maybe he didn't.

He let go of my hair and wrapped his hands around my neck and began to tighten his grip. I was thrilled to be in his clutch, thrilled that a man like him wanted a man like me. I'd succumbed to the virtual stranger in black. I wasn't afraid of death and we could meet our maker together. My airway was constricted and he simply stared into my eyes with the pleasure of a predator. This was it. I'd been suckered into a scene of horror by this man. What would the congregation think? I grabbed his wrists to get his hands off my windpipe, but he was too strong. He became hazy in my view, a fading pair of sinister eyes as I headed toward tranquility. His grip let go and I gasped for air, inhaling as fast as I could, sputtering and glaring at him.

He raised an eyebrow. "You started it."

I slapped him, cutting the corner of his lower lip.

He spit blood on the floor, his eyes never leaving mine. "Not quite the way this goes, Father Superior." He grabbed my hair again and pulled me to a stand.

I cherished the ecstasy of being manhandled.

He was beyond strong and came to a stand beside me. We took up most of the space so there was no escape from him—nor did I want one, anyway. I elbowed him in his side and he fell against the inside of the solid mahogany confessional. The noise reverberated throughout the church.

"What's the matter?" I asked, grinning at him as he pushed up from the bench.

His face told the story of how he handled other men who challenged his dominance. His eyes narrowed and he held his shoulder from where he'd crashed against the wooden interior. It was the only time I'd seen even a shred of evidence he could be hurt.

He jumped toward me and held the back of my neck, bending me forward when he secured one of my arms behind my back.

"This is so much fun," he growled. "I didn't peg you for a violent man, Father. What else are you hiding?"

"We're all hiding something," I hissed, my teeth grinding as he held my arm high behind my back.

"What do you need, Father? Tell me your wildest and dirtiest fantasy," Archer demanded. His free hand searched between my legs for my cock. His grip tightened and I wasn't sure he wouldn't actually break my arm.

"Oh god." I grimaced from the pain.

"You don't need God. I'm all you need," he whispered in my ear, before biting and nipping my earlobe.

"Fuck me," I admitted. "Use me."

He laughed. "If you insist."

Archer spat in one hand, keeping the other on my arm so he could maintain control. His fingers found my hole and he slathered his spit over it. He probed and tested my resistance to his assault, but found none. I had no plan to fight him off. I had my secrets, and he had his, but it was obvious we shared one of them. We wanted each other badly. He frightened and exhilarated me all at once. I fought all the warnings, including my best judgment, and still knew it was a losing battle.

The sound of foil ripping was followed by a cool sensation in my hole. His finger pushed through my barrier and he buried it in one swift movement. It was unpleasant and thrilling at the same time. This wouldn't be sweet and loving. He knew it and I knew it. I doubted Archer even knew tenderness, let alone cared about it.

"If I let go of your arm, are you gonna fight me?" he asked. "Because I'm having this ass. It's your call, Father."

"Own me," I said, bucking my hips. It was only his finger and I was out of control.

"That's what I wanna hear," he responded. He pushed me forward before releasing my arm.

Archer ripped another foil open, and when I glanced behind me, the latex was stretched around his length. I awaited his cock during a brief moment of truce. He could play fair, I noted, but I felt the armistice would be short-lived.

He spat again, rubbing it over the condom. His hand came to my hip; a warning. I prepared for what I thought would be one painful thrust, but it didn't happen that way. He pushed his tip against my hole and waited for me to accept him. I wasn't a novice, but I wasn't overly experienced either, so his approach was appreciated.

"You ready?" he asked, gripping both hips. "I'm going to enjoy the hell out of this."

I was wrong.

He slammed into me in one thrust while I gripped the edges of the bench and inhaled deeply. The pain of forced expansion shot through me but I knew it would pass. In fact, calling it pain was a lie. It was all a part of the act—an act I quite enjoyed. I could play the part of the wounded animal until I was ready to strike.

"God …" I moaned as he filled me.

"You like it, don't you?"

I nodded. "I love it," I admitted, pushing back and taking him as deeply as possible.

His thick cock pounded into me while he held my hips,

pulling me onto him over and over. He rested a foot on top of the bench and changed his angle as he fucked me aggressively. Pressing my lower back, he found his target; his aim was perfection as I began to feel a sensation inside that was the payoff for the initial discomfort.

"Take it, bitch," he hissed, reaching for my hair and pulling my head back. "Cock-lovin' priest." He punched me once, hard, in the spot he'd been pressing on my lower back. It caused me to exhale abruptly, surprising me with its power.

I felt the first slap on an ass cheek. I flinched but didn't say a word. Another smack, but this time with greater force, sending me to my happy place.

"Faster," I panted. "Harder."

He reached for my balls while he drilled me. He yanked them, taking me to the end of pain into pleasure. It was as if he'd read a script about how I needed to be used and knew each step in order.

"Stand up," he barked. He pulled me to a stand by my hair and shoved me against the partition in the small space. He sat on the edge of the bench, glancing at his cock and then at me. "Sit on it facing me."

"And if I don't want to?"

His brow furrowed and he shook his head slowly. "I don't recommend you make that decision."

I pushed him backward and he fell clumsily against the bench. He studied me carefully as I reached behind his neck, joining my hands for support. Using him to keep me upright, I straddled him, my feet flat on the bench beside his thighs. He moved his hands to my neck again as I squatted, ready to receive him.

Archer lifted from the bench and shoved into me quickly. I

would have gasped or grunted my disapproval but I couldn't do either due to his grip on my neck. He eased some of the pressure and allowed me to breathe. I moved up and down, riding him. My dick rubbed against his stomach as we were joined in a frenzy. Two sinners chasing one goal.

"You're good, Father." He grinned when I stared into his light brown eyes. "Such a dirty fucking whore, aren't you?"

He liked talking smack and he was a total badass too, but as we stared into each other's eyes, he slowed down. It looked like he wanted to kiss me.

I slapped him, then spit in his face. "If you're such a great killer, why do you fuck so poorly?"

He smacked me across the face and picked up the pace by holding my hips and forcing me up and down on his cock.

"You're gonna have to try harder to piss me off, Father. I've fucked stronger than you dozens of times." He reached for the sides of my head. He was clearly pissed about the back talk, so I prepared for a potential slap, or worse, maybe a gut punch or two. I received neither. He held the sides of my face and pulled me forward, kissing my neck. He was still inside me but had slowed down, grinding off the bench slower and with more targeted precision.

My hands moved from the back of his head to hold his face. His stubble was rough against my palms. Our wrists were crisscrossed as we moved frantically.

I lifted myself up and down, feverishly working his cock, desperate to find my prostate. I grabbed his hand and shoved it on my dick. I fucked his hand while bouncing on his cock.

Our eyes popped open and locked.

He pumped.

I ground.

"Fuck!" he roared. "Fuckin' hell."

My cock rubbed against his flat stomach, my orgasm seconds away. He was lifting both of us off the bench as he shoved into me harder. His raw strength overpowered me; he held me in a vice-like grip and pumped faster.

He was close.

I was close.

"I'm fucking coming!" he yelled, holding me down and shooting into the condom.

My load shot in time with him yelling and struggling to stay in his seat. "Archer." My low moans announced that I had reached my nirvana. I watched confusion flit across Archer's face before his features returned to his usual scowl.

We gazed at each other's eyes, waiting for one of us to make the first move. Archer slowly pulled himself out of me and I was already missing his touch. He opened his mouth to say something, but didn't.

The wave of regret and guilt was no match to the mind-blowing connection we had shared. He picked up his clothes, putting them on one by one. He opened the curtain and started walking away, but paused after a few steps. He looked back, staring directly at my face. What I wouldn't give to read what was on his mind. Archer shook his head before disappearing into the shadows.

Sixteen: The Reaper

It was the wee hours and I was left with nothing but my own thoughts. I caressed my chest where Father Saint James's hands had been. What we shared was rough. I was surprised he'd kept up with me. He wasn't as fragile as I'd thought. He was strong, both his will and his strength. He told me he could've handled those men who attacked him and I felt like a fool for not believing him. He could go toe-to-toe with any of the men I knew and possibly win, and I had suspected he was still holding back a little.

Father Saint James was a puzzle needing to be solved.

I waited in the dark for the morning to come. My appetite for Father Saint James was stronger than before we'd fucked. Hearing my name come out of his mouth when he came was better than I could have imagined. It was so arousing and I came harder than ever, placing me in unfamiliar territory. I've never craved seconds before, I didn't even know what they were like. I was always done after the first bang—pun intended. But with my priest, I couldn't wait to do it all over again.

Maybe the assignment in Monaco was exactly what I needed to recalibrate and refocus on the ultimate destination, an

SIXTEEN: THE REAPER

ending with a dull conclusion. There were a lot bigger things than Father Saint James. And if I was to succeed, he needed to be gone. Out of sight, out of mind kind of bullshit.

And yet, he was the last thing on my mind before my eyelids grew heavy and I succumbed to sleep.

The buzzing of my alarm rattled me awake. It took a second for my brain to register where I was. I'd fallen asleep on the hard floor and my back was paying for it. I grabbed my phone from the floor where I'd left it the night before, frowning at the lack of response from Tobias. My worry grew, but I shrugged it off. *One more assignment*, I told myself. This would be over soon.

***

Monaco was the unlikeliest of places for a mission like mine, but here I was, in the lobby of a five-diamond hotel in the heart of Monte Carlo, dressed in white denim pants that were so tight they looked painted on. It was a wonder my balls were able to fit with this cut. A pink shirt was tucked into my pants under a navy blue sports jacket, and finished with lambskin loafers. I could hardly recognize myself, but I guessed that was the point. You had to dress the part to blend in.

"*Bonjour, monsieur,*" a skinny man wearing a white shirt and a maroon vest with gold embroidery greeted me when I walked up to the counter. Behind him was a floor-to-ceiling mirrored wall, giving me a vantage point of what was behind me.

"*Bonjour,*" I said, pushing the bridge of my sunglasses. I leaned on the counter when I reached him.

His name was Sebastian, according to his golden name plate. "American?" he asked, giggling.

"What gave me away?" I teased, flashing my brightest smile. "Was it my clothes?" I stepped back so he could check me out.

He shook his head.

"No? Was it my hair? Gotta be my hair." I finger-combed my well-styled blond hair. "Tell me it's my hair."

He placed his hand over his lips. Another shake of his head. Sebastian was definitely gay and I knew then that I had him captive. "It's your accent," he explained.

"My sexy American accent?" I wet my lips with my tongue, leaning closer.

"It is very sexy indeed," he admitted. Redness crept over his pale skin. "Eh … are you checking in?"

"Yes, my name is Peter Robinson," I answered.

We were interrupted by an obnoxious voice. "Hold it, please." A middle-aged man, about six feet tall, rushed to the gold-plated elevator behind me. Max Lancaster, my target. He beamed at the person manning the elevator. "Do you speak English?"

"A little, monsieur," a man wearing a uniform like Sebastian's answered.

My eyes fixated on his mouth. Not because there was something remarkable about his wrinkled lips and yellow teeth. No, I was focused on his lips so I could make out what he was saying. "You people should learn," Max said. "Eighth floor, do you understand that? Eighth. Floor!" The doors closed and he was gone.

"Monsieur?" Sebastian asked, bringing my attention to his smiling face. He'd been appraising me since the moment I entered the luxury hotel. It was the reason why I chose to stand in his line. "Should we check you in?" His attempt to speak English was accompanied by pointing to his computer.

SIXTEEN: THE REAPER

"Pardon," I said in apology. *"Oui, s'il vous plaît."* I was no expert in French, but my limited ability was enough to get me by.

Pleased that I spoke his native tongue, he proceeded to tell me things about the hotel but I tuned out and went into planning mode. Sebastian's lips kept moving, but my mind was going one hundred miles per hour. *"Sixieme etage,"* he said.

"Did you say sixth floor?" I asked.

"Oui."

I employed my Casanova mask, intent on charming my way to the eighth floor. I curled my index finger, asking him to meet me halfway. "Sebastian," I said. "I love that name. It fits you. What does your girlfriend call you?" I asked, dragging the tip of my tongue around my lips.

"No girlfriend," he answered, appearing somewhat flustered. His cheeks blushed a darker shade of red, but he never broke eye contact.

"Boyfriend?" I asked.

"No boyfriend," he answered, looking down at his joined hands. "I had a boyfriend before, but no more."

"Aww," I sympathized. Thankfully, the waiting guests behind me switched to another line. "Look at me," I whispered, my voice raspy and deep. I removed my sunglasses and met Sebastian's eyes. "It's a shame. A man like you deserves to be cherished. Do you understand that word?" I doubled down and reached for his hand, placing mine over his. "Real shame." I winked.

"Merci," he said, clearing his throat. "Here's your key, monsieur." He slid a golden key card into a black envelope.

I reached for his hand, stopping him. "I was hoping to be on the eighth floor," I said. "It's very special to me. You see, my late husband—" Sebastian's eyes sparkled in delight "—and I used to stay on the eighth floor. But he passed away last year, and I'm trying to visit all the places we loved. It's helping me to move on, you know." I didn't know how revisiting a place helped someone move on, but Sebastian seemed to be buying my story.

"I'm sorry, monsieur, but the top floor is for special guests."

"You don't think I'm special?" I caressed the back of his hand with my knuckles.

Sebastian was unable to hide the effect my touch had on him when goosebumps appeared on his forearm.

"So, Sebastian …" I trailed off, waiting. "Gosh, I love that name." I drew small circles on his wrist with my index finger, while he shivered under my touch. "Are you saying you don't think I'm special?" I frowned, the feigned look of hurt on my face intensifying. "Here I am thinking we were making a personal connection."

Sebastian glanced to his sides before leaning closer to me, wheels turning in his head. "Let me check one more time," he whispered. He brought his attention back to the computer, his fingers frantically typing.

"Take your time. I got all day, baby." I didn't, but a few more minutes of flirting wouldn't hurt anybody.

His face lit up. "It looks like we have one room left."

"Am I special enough to have it?"

He smiled. *"Oui."*

I reached for his hand and kissed the back of it. "Thank you, Sebastian. You're my hero."

He handed me a new room card and I tapped his hand one more time for good measure.

"See you," he called.

I looked back and winked. *That was fucking easy.* I picked up my bag and walked to the elevator. I made eye contact with Sebastian, who no doubt was watching my every move. I smiled and waved just as the elevator door closed.

A guy wedged his hand between the closing elevator door, forcing it open once again. "Sorry about that." A family stepped inside the now-very-crowded elevator.

I ignored them, pressing the button for the eighth floor.

"Do you mind pressing six, please?" the man, who I assumed was the father, asked.

Instead of saying anything, I moved away from the control and leaned back against the mirrored walls, putting my sunglasses back on. "I do mind," I said. *I'm not your fucking bellboy.*

The man shook his head, angrily pressing the sixth-floor button himself.

Six floors later, the elevator door opened and the family got out. The man glanced back at me, a look of disgust on his face.

I flipped him the bird before reaching over with my shoe to close the door.

Walking through the ornate hall of the eighth floor, I counted the number of rooms and noted the distance from the staircase and my room. Behind one of these doors was my target, and the sooner I accomplished this assignment, the less time I had to spend in this city. I went to the end of the hallway, where an arrangement of colorful fresh flowers sat in a glass vase. The water level was three-quarters of the way up. It would take four to five days before someone replaced these flowers, at the very least replenished the water. Plenty of time.

I grabbed the green dime-sized clip-on camera from my pocket and faced it toward the hallway, including the elevator. Once satisfied it was stable and hidden, I found my room. I turned The Firm-assigned phone on and opened the camera's app. "Perfect!" All I had to do was wait.

After stripping to my boxer briefs, I opened my laptop and clicked the link leading me to the camera outside. I set it on the table, before grabbing a small bottle of purple-label whiskey from the mini bar, polishing its content and reaching for another.

Hours went by and Max Lancaster still hadn't made an appearance. I grabbed my personal cell out of my suitcase, going straight to the video feed of Father Saint James. Jerking off was in order, and any reel with Father Saint James would suffice. But because God was funny like that, he chose the perfect time to have the man come out of room 815.

I pulled out the blank key card, exactly like the one Sebastian had given me. "Zero has this key's code so all you have to do is give her the room number," El Jefe had told me before I left Boston. I scrolled through my contacts, pressing Zero's name.

"Do you have his room number?" Zero asked. She was one of the best hackers The Firm had and she could penetrate through any firewall.

"Room 815," I said.

"Done," she said after two minutes. I wished I knew Zero better. If there was one person who could access the list, it would be her. "Anything else?" she asked.

"Umm." The words were on the tip of my tongue, but I couldn't bring myself to ask.

"What is it?"

"Nothing," I said, ending the call before I did something I'd regret.

Seventeen: The Priest

I stood in front of the mirror, admiring the scratches marking my neck and body, tracing every purple and red spot dotting my arms. They were graphic reminders of my encounter with Archer, evidence that there was pleasure in pain. It could be argued that one couldn't exist without the other. How could one truly experience pleasure without going through pain? I traced each bruise, a badge I would temporarily wear until the high of last night dissipated. It had been exhilarating, awakening my senses. I felt alive.

I counted to a hundred, willing myself to crash to the ground where I'd spent a considerable amount of time. Reality began to knock me off my feet. I had a mission to perform and a flock of parishioners to lead. Last night couldn't and shouldn't happen again. It was a slippery slope leading me back to failure, which I couldn't afford, no matter what the reward was.

Once sobered from the drug that was Archer, I got dressed to start my day, hoping no one could sense the sins of last night. I grabbed my phone sitting on top of the dresser before heading out of my room. I dialed Andrew's number and, like dozens of times before, it went straight to voice mail. I ended the call and stared at my wall. "I need you, Andrew."

My open laptop greeted me when I made it into the office. I was frustrated by the lack of progress with the USB. It had been a while since I'd received it and I was nowhere near guessing the password. Factoring in the fact that I'd yet to hear from the church about my assignment, I was starting to panic about my mission, worrying if they'd changed their minds. What would happen if they did? Where would I go? My mind was inundated with what-if scenarios. I was in a trance when I exited the house.

"Hi, Father!" Tim burst out of the church and scared me sideways. "I'm sorry. I didn't mean to scare you like that," he said, removing his baseball cap.

"I'm okay." I waved it off. "Just didn't get enough sleep." It wasn't entirely a lie. I'd been operating on under four hours of sleep since I arrived in Boston. It'd been two weeks and I had yet to hear from the church about the details of my mission. How long did they plan to keep me here?

"We've all been there. New city and all. You'll adjust soon," he assured me.

"I hope so," I said. "What are you up to today?"

"I'm heading to a baseball game. The Yankees are in town." He pulled a ticket from his pocket. He wore a navy blue New York Yankees jersey on top of his jeans.

"By yourself?" I asked.

He nodded. "Yup."

I admired people who could go to those kinds of events alone. I'd never been able to. Andrew and I were inseparable when we were kids, and I didn't have time when I was an adult. I dedicated my entire adulthood to school, the seminary, and the mission. I sometimes wondered how it felt to have fun.

The thought of fun brought me back to last night. I had a different kind of life, but I wondered how it would feel to go to the game with someone. Someone like Archer. I shook off the idea. Moving forward, I had one goal: my mission.

"Are you sure you're fine?" Tim surveyed my solemn face.

"Yes, go ahead and have fun. Eat a hotdog for me," I said, playfully shooing him away.

"Want me to bring you one?" he asked.

"That's so kind of you, but no. I'll stick to my boring salad."

I entered the church after Tim left and my eyes wandered to the confession booth. Reminders of Archer were everywhere. Concentrating was going to be harder than I realized.

My phone vibrated. When I glanced at the screen, I was stunned. I blinked, making sure my eyes weren't playing tricks on me. It wouldn't be the first time. I accepted the call and brought the phone closer to my ear. "Andrew?" My question was met with nothing but sequential beeps. "Andrew!" My voice echoed through the church. I quickly checked the screen. "Andrew!" The call disconnected.

"Good morning, Father," Jessica greeted, a little cautiously.

I jumped, not realizing anyone else was inside.

She paused from hanging a bouquet of flowers and looked at me curiously, her eyes furrowed. "Is everything all right?" Jessica climbed down from the small ladder, heading toward me. "Who's Andrew?"

"Huh?" I staggered back, disoriented by the call from my brother. Where was he? Was he in trouble? Questions flooded my brain. I wasn't going to admit it, but Andrew's disappearance had me in a tailspin. It was one of the reasons I ultimately failed my last mission in Albuquerque.

"Are you sick? You're sweating." She rushed to a pew and

grabbed a box of tissues, pulled out three sheets and handed them to me. "Let's sit over there." She ushered me into the first row, her eyes never leaving mine. She took the soaked tissue from my hand after I wiped my forehead and cheeks. "Do you want me to get you a cup of water?"

"No, thank you," I managed to say, finally. I had to tell her something to explain my reaction moments ago.

"So …" Jessica set the box of tissues aside. "Who's Andrew? I heard you scream his name."

I hadn't realized I was yelling. "He's my brother," I answered. The fog that enveloped my brain lifted; I could see clearly. "He called but I couldn't hear anything. I didn't mean to disrupt what you were doing." I looked around trying to figure out who else had heard me.

"Oh, don't worry about it," Jessica said, perhaps reading my mind. "It's just me since Tim left." She stood and headed to the bin to discard the used tissues.

"I saw him leaving. I didn't know he was a baseball fan." I grabbed the box of Kleenex and placed it back at the end of the pew. I needed to be moving. Sitting around wouldn't help.

"He's a huge Yankees fan. I have yet to see him without some sort of Yankees gear. He's got jackets, hats, and T-shirts. He's like a walking commercial for them," she said, chuckling. "I don't know how I feel about working with a Yankees fan."

"I take it you're a Red Sox fan?" I asked, thankful that she'd dropped the subject of Andrew.

"My whole family."

This was the first time she'd mentioned her family, and I was genuinely interested. I loved getting to know the people in my parish. It was both my strength and my weakness. *"You care too much about these people,"* one of my superiors once told me. *"You have to create a division to separate you from the parish and your mission."* I used to believe that the parish and my mission were the same, but my recent experience made me reconsider. Maybe that was what I needed to succeed here in Boston: detach myself from everyone and focus on the mission. *Keep my eyes on the prize.* It was easier said than done, especially here with Jessica, awaiting a response. "Tell me about them," I said.

Jessica beamed. She pulled her phone out of her pocket, scrolling through images. "This is my husband, Clark." She pointed to a handsome man with reddish hair standing next to her in a photo. "And that's our daughter, Lucy," she said, pointing at the little girl with a pixie haircut on Clark's shoulders.

"You have a beautiful family," I said. Everyone in the photograph had their Red Sox attire on and stood smiling in front of Fenway Park. "My brother and I used to watch them every spring."

"Oh yeah? I didn't know you were also a baseball fan." She pocketed her phone.

"Big time. One of our favorite pictures was taken at that same spot before he went to the seminary. He used to say, 'Always go back to this picture whenever you're lost,' before he left." It had taken me out of some dark times, when I was alone and felt like giving up. Our smiling faces reminded me that I was someone's family. I was loved. I missed my brother.

"Is he a priest as well?" Jessica asked.

I nodded. "A well-respected one." Andrew was one of the best and the Church knew it. "If I could be half as good as he is, I would consider myself lucky."

"I've only known you for a couple weeks and I can tell you're

SEVENTEEN: THE PRIEST

amazing. You're kind and charismatic," Jessica assured me. "Don't sell yourself short."

"You're too kind. Sometimes I feel like I don't know what I'm doing. I feel lost," I admitted. No guidance. No one to talk to. I was alone.

"Well, remember what your brother used to say ..." She pulled her phone out of her pocket, waving the photograph of her family in front of the Fenway Park gate.

"Always go back to this picture whenever you're lost," I said, chuckling.

"That's right. I have to finish up. Are you sure you're okay?"

"You know what? I am now. Thank you, Jessica."

"You're welcome, Father."

She went back to hanging flowers and I was left standing in the middle of the church. A thought began to crystallize.

Always go back to this picture whenever you're lost.

I hurried back to the house, heading straight to the office. I fired up my laptop, and while I waited I scrolled through my favorite images on my phone until I found the picture of Andrew and I. We were standing in the same spot as Jessica's family, in front of Fenway Park's iconic facade, where the year it opened was etched. I slid the USB drive into its port, and when the pop-up notification asked for the password, I studied the image once again. I keyed in *FenwayPark1912* and waited.

Just like that, the file opened.

Shocked, all I could do was stare at the open file containing three folders.

Is this from you, Andrew?

Eighteen: The Reaper

Terraces of old buildings with brown terracotta-tiled roofs lined the hillsides of Monte Carlo. Multimillion-dollar mega yachts bobbed at the marina, peppering the turquoise water of the Mediterranean. Because beaches were a high-priced commodity in this part of the world, luxury residential areas hugged the city's coastline. I wasn't gonna lie, Monaco was the shit people made it out to be. It screamed money, a haven for those who had too much.

I paced alongside the interior window of my hotel room, waiting for notifications of any movements in the hallway from the camera I'd hidden, but aside from the occasional member of the cleaning staff making their rounds, Max 'will-be-dead-soon' Lancaster was yet to return to his suite.

Hours had gone by and my boredom was at an all-time high, and there wasn't a fucking thing I could do about it. It was a waiting game until the real action began. I reached for my bag, pulling Max's file from it. According to the back of the photo, more than twenty women were reported missing and he was linked to every single one of them. People who'd done a quarter of the awful things he did were rotting in jail. The difference between them and Max? Money. Loads of it. The man was a fucking monster.

It took one to know one.

***

Twelve Years Ago

The glass of my bedroom window rattled from the loud roar of a motorcycle passing by. The sound dissipated, but came back after a minute, where it halted right outside. It sounded like a Harley. My fascination with bikes had grown these past few years, and I found myself researching everything about them, even going as far as memorizing the sound of each brand. That distinctive growl was, without a doubt, a Harley. My interest didn't end with motorcycles. It bled into cars and trucks. I could easily tell what the makes and models of vehicles were from their sound.

I hopped off the bed and looked out the window. A man wearing all black, including his helmet, sat on the idle bike. I was right, it was a Harley. His head was cocked toward my window. His face was hidden behind a black visor, but I knew he was staring at me. Do I know this person?

My cell beeped with a text from my friend Luke. We were in the same class and played basketball together. We weren't any good, but we decided to join the team because there weren't many activities to keep teenage boys occupied in our small town. It was exciting at first. Sharing a locker room with a bunch of jocks was fun, but that got old real fast when I realized that none of them were my type.

Still wanna go out tonight? *his text read. It was my eighteenth birthday, and our new friend Wolf had invited both of us to a party to celebrate my adulthood.*

After typing Hell yeah, *I headed downstairs to ask my grandparents, pausing on the last step when I overheard their conversation.*

"Where do you think she is?" *Grandma asked Grandpa. I didn't mean to eavesdrop, but my curiosity always won whenever the subject of my parents came up.* "I can't for the love of me think of any reason why a mother would leave a beautiful boy like that. Poor kid. Orphaned at such a young age."

"He's not an orphan, he has you and me," *Grandpa said. It was the truth. They'd raised me, and I couldn't be luckier to have such wonderful people in my life.*

"I know that. But we're old. What if something happens to us? Who will look after him? He's been through so much already." *Grandma's voice broke as she spoke.*

I cornered the living room, hiding behind the wall in order to get a glimpse of them. They were sitting next to each other, drinking tea. They enjoyed tea after dinner. Grandma stared into her porcelain cup, tracing the delicate edge of the matching saucer, which held a small slice of the birthday cake she had baked for me. You couldn't miss the agony of losing her son and daughter-in-law engraved on her face. This was one of the very rare occasions they crumbled.

"Do you think she's still alive?" *she asked, looking into Grandpa's eyes.*

I wondered what hurt the most: her being dead, or to know she was alive and chose to abandon me ten years ago?

"I don't know," *Grandpa answered. He rested his oversized reading glasses on top of his gray hair, before reaching over to hold Grandma's hand.* "It's been ten years, and as much as I hate to admit it ..." *He took a deep breath before kissing her forehead. I'd never seen two people more in love than my grands.* "I don't believe that she would last long without seeing her baby boy. She loved that kid. They both did."

EIGHTEEN: THE REAPER

How could a sentence pack so much sorrow? My parents loved me, but I couldn't remember how that felt. Their voices were faint whispers, and the only reason I remembered their faces was because of the photos my grandma kept above the fireplace. My chest tightened, pulling a soft sob out of my throat.

They both glanced in my direction, Grandma wiping away her tears. She stood and rushed toward me, caging me with her embrace. She didn't say anything. She didn't need to.

Grandpa led us to the dining table.

"Um ... Grandma?" I asked, after the surge of sadness that had rendered me speechless passed.

"What is it, my love?" She loosened her hold on me, reaching up to cup my face. She wiped the streaks of tears from my face, combing my hair with her fingers. "Did you need something?"

I nodded. "My friends are going to this party and I was hoping to go with them?"

"Have we met these friends?" Grandpa asked. "They're not drinking, are they?" He looked up at the wall clock, perhaps wondering what kind of party started at eleven o'clock at night. They weren't strict, but it was way past my bedtime. "Is Luke going too?"

"Yes, he's going," I said.

"Who else?" Grandma asked.

"His name is Wolf. Luke and I met him recently," I answered, crossing my fingers. "He's a cool guy," I added.

"Wolf?" Grandma asked.

I nodded. "We call him Wolf. That's his nickname."

My grandparents exchanged glances, Grandpa shaking his head slightly.

"Please," I said. "I don't want my birthday to end just yet. Please? You said it yourself, Grandpa, I only get to be eighteen once, so I

better enjoy it."

I held my breath waiting for their response. They worried about me. How could they not after the death of my dad and Mom's disappearance?

Grandpa blew out a breath, surrendering. "Be back before two," he said, reaching over to wrap his arm around Grandma's shoulders. "Remember ..." He trailed off. "We don't sleep until you're safely home." They told me that a lot. I used to think it was a ploy to guilt me into staying in, but I was proven wrong when I once arrived home late without telling them where I was. They never gave me grief about it. Knowing they were worried about me was worse than any punishment they could dish out. It was effective too, because I'd never stayed out past ten. But today called for a celebration. I was finally an adult, and there was no better way to commemorate than to stay out late.

"This guy—" Grandpa started.

"His name is Wolf." Grandma chuckled.

"This Wolf. He's a good guy, right?"

"He is." I didn't know a lot about him, but he seemed like a solid person. He'd taken us to the movies and even taught me how to shoot a gun. They didn't need to know that. He was a bit older than us at thirty, but he was very cool. I wanted to be like him when I was his age.

"Okay," Grandpa said.

"Okay, like, yes?" I asked, grinning.

"We trust your judgment," Grandma said. "Don't grow up too soon." She pulled me to her petite frame, kissing the side of my face repeatedly.

Grandpa joined us and kissed the top of my head.

"I'll be safe." I grabbed my car keys from the counter then headed toward the door.

EIGHTEEN: THE REAPER

"Take a coat!" she called out.

"Got it!" I yelled.

The man I'd seen from upstairs was still watching our house, but immediately drove off, disrupting the quiet evening, when I got into my car. That was odd.

"Where are we?" Luke asked, looking around the street the moment we parked my car.

"These are the directions Wolf gave us," I said, glancing at the handwritten note and the rusty metal gate of an old warehouse. The directions he'd given us took us twenty miles away from Belfast. It was an old shipping container storage yard by Penobscot Bay. The surroundings were damp and shrouded in fog; we couldn't see more than twenty feet in front of us.

"Are you sure?" Luke grabbed the paper and squinted at the scrawled directions. "This is it ... but why would he ask us to come here? It's a fucking dump." He pointed at the dilapidated building riddled with rusting holes. "That shit is falling apart."

He was right, but there had to be a reason Wolf sent us here. "I don't know," I said. "Wanna leave?" I hoped he'd say yes; I had a bad feeling about this place. I hated to admit it, but it was creeping me out.

"Maybe it's a surprise for your birthday?" Luke suggested, excitement creeping into his voice. "He's cool like that."

Well, that was a possibility. "You think so?" I didn't really think it was, but what did we have to lose? We'd traveled this far so we might as well stay.

"Yeah. Let's go." He jumped out of the car and I followed.

"Hello?" I called, my voice echoing. "Wolf?"

"Why is it so dark?" Luke asked. We used our cell phones to light our path.

"I dunno."

The gate was locked, so we jumped over the fence and made our way to the middle of the empty warehouse. The eerie quiet made me regret my decision to ever come here.

"We should leave," Luke said, his usual playful voice laced with worry.

"Yeah, let's go," I agreed.

Five men double our size appeared out of nowhere and blocked our way. "Leaving so soon?" *one of them asked.*

"Who the hell are you?" *I asked. My heart raced, terror taking me over. Two of the guys grabbed Luke's arm.* "Hey, get your hands off him!"

"Get the fuck off me," *Luke yelled.* "HELP! HELP!"

"Shut up, you little bitch." *One of the guys hit Luke's head with a gun and he crumpled to the ground.*

"Luke!" *I moved to rush to my friend but was grabbed by the collar. I tried wiggling away without success. The man pulled my hands behind me, I was no match for his strength.* "Luke! LUKE!" *He lay still; unconscious. This had to be a nightmare. This wasn't happening.*

I closed my eyes, shaking my head repeatedly. When I opened them, I spotted a shadow moving behind the two goons standing over Luke. "Help!" *I screamed at them.*

My yell for help earned a punch in the gut and my body attempted to fold over. If it wasn't for the man holding my hands behind my back, I would have been on the ground too.

I was yanked up, and as the new arrival passed by the light shining through a broken window, I recognized him immediately.

Hope bloomed when our eyes met. "Help," *I muttered again.* "Wolf, please?"

Wolf stopped next to the man with the gun. They looked at each other and fist-bumped.

EIGHTEEN: THE REAPER

All hope evaporated; my world darkened. "What the fuck, man?" I gasped. "Who the hell are they?"

Wolf grinned. "These are my friends," he said.

"Why are you doing this? We didn't do anything to you." I wanted to punch him, but the guy yanked my hands back with such force, I winced.

"I brought you here for this." Wolf neared the wall. He flipped the light switch on, revealing three guys from our school lying in a pool of blood. They'd been shot.

"Oh my fucking god! Oh my fucking god!" I cried. "Please let us go, we won't say anything!" The man holding me forced me to kneel. "Don't kill us, please. I'm begging you." Images of my grandparents floated in my head. They couldn't lose their grandson as well.

"We're not gonna kill you," Wolf insisted. He walked closer, holding a box with a gun inside. "Remember this gun?"

"No," I answered, shaking my head.

"This was the one you practiced with," Wolf said, handing the box to one of his men.

"What does that have to do with anything?"

"Oh, you naive little boy." Wolf nodded to one of the guys. Everything moved in slow motion when I realized he was wearing gloves as he took the gun out of the box. "Any final words to your friend?"

"No!" I cried. "No, please don't do this."

The man holding the gun stood over Luke's body, aiming it at my friend's head.

Bang.

"Luke!" I screamed. Then pain reverberated from the back of my head and I knew no more. My world went dark.

Wailing sirens dragged me from a nightmare. Relieved that I was awake, I rubbed the back of my throbbing head. I blinked, trying to clear the fog from my brain. I wasn't at home.

Everything came rushing back in feverish droves and panic took over my senses.

The men.

Wolf.

The dead bodies.

Luke.

"Luke?" I called, my voice hoarse. I pushed off the cold, dirt-covered floor and looked around. He was only a few feet away, but my brain still felt disconnected from my body and the distance felt like miles.

I scrambled over, collapsed next to him, and grabbed his hand. "Luke?" I asked helplessly. I knew he was gone, but I didn't want it to be true. "I'm so sorry," I murmured to his lifeless body.

The sirens were so loud, echoing through the old warehouse, piercing my ears and causing me to wince.

I had to get out of here. Seeing the gun a few inches away, I dropped Luke's hand and picked up the gun to get rid of it just as tires screeched outside, followed by the popping of car doors and feet pounding on gravel.

I was surrounded. It was just a dream.

The warehouse doors flew open, the flashing lights caused me to lift my hand to shield my face.

"Drop your weapon!" the cop said.

I lowered my hand and stared at the gun as if it was an alien object. Oh god. This was bad. "I didn't do it," I croaked. Shaking my head, I cried, "It wasn't me!"

"Drop your weapon and put your hands over your head where I can see them."

I tossed the gun Wolf had used to shoot Luke and raised my hands.

EIGHTEEN: THE REAPER

"It wasn't me. You have to believe me. Luke is my friend," I pleaded when one of the officers cuffed my hands and pushed me forward.

"What the fuck happened here?" one of the officers murmured.

"It wasn't me. I was set up."

I was taken into custody that evening. All the evidence pointed to me. The police never found Wolf, and the only person who could vouch for my innocence was Luke ... and he was dead.

***

I was dragged back to the present when my monitor pinged, notifying me of activity outside. I focused my attention on the screen and watched as Max walked down the hallway to his room. He had his arm draped over a woman's shoulders and was whispering in her ear. I zeroed in on his lips.

"Ready to have some fun?" he'd said to her.

She nodded, giggling.

Max tickled her side, before slapping her ass as they entered his room.

Damn it. I was hoping to get this shit over with so I could go back home, but I couldn't do that with a possible witness. I was about to close the computer when the same woman rushed out of Max's room, barefoot. She clutched her coat and shoes to her chest, yelling behind her.

"Well, what do we have here?" I whispered.

Max followed, stopping when guests came out of the elevators, before quickly retreating to his room.

I grabbed my phone, redialing Zero's number.

"Are you ready?" she asked.

"Whenever you are."

"Let me log in to their server." Zero's plan was to get

into the hotel's security server to replace the surveillance with a recording, deleting the actual footage of me entering and leaving the target's room. "I'm in," she said after a few moments.

"Give me an hour," I said. I didn't need that much time, I could do the assignment in five minutes, but I planned on having fun with this motherfucker.

"Good luck," she said before hanging up.

I grabbed the vial of Propofol from my bag, drawing a syringe full for my new best friend. After replacing the paraphernalia into the duffel, I slid into my leather gloves, popped on a hat to hide my face, and headed out to pay someone a little visit.

Max was sitting in a plush armchair jacking his nearly limp miniature cock when I snuck into his room. He wore a virtual reality headset, allowing me to enter without being noticed. His frantic hand jerked his meat while he panted, sticking his tongue out like a maniac.

I silently approached him, even going as far as to hold my breath, when I stepped carefully over the cords connected to the tripod that was set up to record his victims.

"That's right," he groaned. "Take my fat cock."

Fighting hard not to chuckle, I stood behind him.

Max tensed mere seconds before the needle glided into his oily neck with precision. "What the f—" He attempted to stand and grabbed at his neck, but my special cocktail had him slumped to the floor before he could.

I set about moving him to the bed, tying his arms and legs to the corner posts with rope. After repositioning Max's tripod, I aimed the camera at him. He was out, and completely naked, when I poured a bucket of icy water on his head.

EIGHTEEN: THE REAPER

He gasped in surprise. "Who the fuck are you? What are you doing here?" He squirmed, wriggled, and twitched as he tried to free himself, but he was wasting his energy. "What are you gonna do to me?" His eyes darted to the door. "HELP!" Max thrust his face forward, headbutting my left eye.

"Fucker!" That was going to give me a black eye. I gagged his mouth with a dirty sock I had found lying on the floor. "You yell one more time and I'mma shoot your mouth with this." I tapped my pistol against his pimpled nose, causing his eyes to widen. "And your breath smells like shit, rotten like your sorry ass." The last statement was irrelevant, but I was petty like that. "Now, are you gonna cooperate?"

He bobbed his head, mumbling a muffled "yes."

I pulled the sock out of his mouth, tossing it to the side. "Now, do you remember these women?" I tugged his hair, forcing him to look at the images I had in my hand.

"I don't know them," he said. "SOMEONE'S TRYIN' TO KILL ME!" he screamed.

Motherfucker. I should've known. I swung my gun at his face, where it thudded against his eyebrow. His skin broke from the force, blood splattered the white pillowcase. "You fucking scream one more time and you're dead." I was giving him false hope, since he was dead the moment my feet touched the ground in Monaco.

"Okay, okay," Max said, the last of his bravery slipping away. "Name your price. Whatever you need, just don't kill me."

I loved it when they begged. "I don't need your money." They were all the same, believing their fat wallets could save them.

"Then what do you want?"

"These women, where did—"

"I don't know them!"

I slapped him with the back of my gloved hand. "You interrupt me one more time and we'll see what happens. I'm gonna ask you again, and I want you to think before you answer."

The pathetic wimp nodded like a trained dog.

"Look at these women." I held the images in front of him again. "Where are they?" I raised my gun when Max's mouth opened and desperation filled his eyes. "Remember my warning," I reminded him. "Think carefully. Take your time."

He stared at the photos, squinting through the blood and sweat dripping into his eye. He shook his head. "How would I know? I don't recognize any of them."

I narrowed my eyes and twitched my trigger finger, making my deadly intent clear. "Think harder."

He shut his eyes, shaking his sweaty head, his hair clinging to his forehead. "Okay, I will tell you."

"Good call." I walked back to the tripod and pressed record. "Where did you hide them?" I then enumerated each woman's name.

Max was breathing hard, tears cascading down his bony cheeks. "Oh my god," he said.

"What did you do to them, Max?" I repeated, glancing at the nightstand clock. He was royally testing my patience with his bullshit.

He stared at the camera and I zoomed in on his face. "I killed them," he confessed. "All of them."

"Where did you bury them?"

Max sobbed, a pitiful sound accompanied by tears and snot.

"Max!"

"A cement factory in Arizona."

EIGHTEEN: THE REAPER

"Arizona is big. I'm gonna need you to be more specific."

He nodded, telling the camera about their exact location. As he spoke, I grabbed the hotel-issued shower cap from the bathroom, stood on a chair underneath the room's smoke detector, and covered it with the cap.

I lit a cigarette, taking a lungful of smoke. "See how easy that was?" It never failed to amaze me what people like Max would do or say when faced with false hope about their inevitable end. Did he really think there was a way he could confess himself out of this shit? "Any final words for your fans?" I asked as I attached the silencer to the barrel of my gun.

"You said you'd let me go!" Max bucked his body up and down, tugging his roped hands in another desperate attempt to escape the conclusion of his story. Thankfully these beds were bolted to the wall and floor.

"You know there's only one way this ends. See you in hell, fucker." I ended the video with the muffled shot and Max's bloody face in the frame.

One last thing left to do. I directed my attention to the MacBook hooked to the video camera. The screen brightened when I tapped it. Within a few clicks, I uploaded the recording to his prized site on the dark web where he'd posted his grisly snuff videos. After clicking publish, I flushed my cigarette down the toilet and headed out.

I fired a text to Zero to let her know it was over: *Done.* One word. Max didn't deserve anything else.

Nineteen: The Priest

I've got to get some sleep. After consuming my tenth cup of coffee, I resumed examining the files with a fine-tooth comb. At first glance, nothing was remarkable about the photos and the grid with names and random numbers. Photos of me during the last two weeks of my mission in Albuquerque and my arrival in Boston filled my laptop screen. In many of the pictures I was alone, while the majority included parishioners in the background. All of these images looked like candid shots, taken by someone I hadn't noticed. The one inside my house was unnerving, because it was clearly taken from outside.

Feeling violated, I quickly stood up and closed all of my curtains and made sure my windows were locked.

How did Andrew get these photos? Why would he send them to me? What was I missing?

A soft knock on the door startled me, making my heart thump painfully against my ribs. After seeing dozens of photos of myself, my paranoia was off the charts and fueling my already high anxiety. I glanced at the clock and groaned. I was late for the confession. I'd been consumed by trying to piece the puzzle together and had completely forgotten about my obligations.

"Father Saint James?" Jessica called from outside, before she knocked again.

I tightened my robe and headed to the living room. "Hi, Jessica. I'm running a little behind. My apologies," I said, hiding behind the slightly opened door. Priests were modest and I wasn't about to let the church staff see me with just a robe on.

"That's okay. No one's here yet so you're fine. I just wanted to check on you and let you know that your schedule has been updated. Make sure you check it." She smiled. "I won't keep you. See you shortly?"

"Yes. Thanks for this." I waved the small stack of envelopes before closing the door. I pulled my phone from my robes and opened my calendar. Grimacing at the back-to-back meetings that filled the rest of the day, I exhaled an exhausted sigh. Spending an all-nighter staring at the computer wasn't a smart choice considering how hectic the day was.

I beelined to the office and pulled the USB from my laptop. This would have to wait.

***

"That was the last one," Jessica said once the principal from the affiliated elementary school exited the church. He'd personally dropped off the invitation for an upcoming fundraiser. It was our first time meeting, and although he was kind, he kept stressing the importance of my presence, and insisted I would help generate higher funds for the school. No pressure.

"Thank goodness." I twisted in my seat to face her.

"You must be tired." She sat in the pew behind me, checking

off a list on the notepad I had gifted her.

"A little. Nothing a cup of coffee can't fix," I said. At this point, someone might as well inject caffeine directly into my veins.

"Oh, you want me to make you a pot?" Jessica rose to her feet, but I raised my hand, stopping her.

"No, it's okay," I said.

"Are you sure? I don't mind."

"I'm sure. It's probably not a good idea to have another this late." There was still light outside, but the sun was on its way down. One advantage of keeping busy was it kept me from obsessing about those images, and a certain man tattooed in my mind. I wondered where he'd been. It'd been a few days since I'd seen him.

The church door opened and a man entered wearing a black hoodie and black jeans. He marched past us, stopping in front of the confession booth. He didn't say a word, nor did he acknowledge us.

My heart stopped. Excitement filled me, but I kept my exhilaration at bay, maintaining a neutral expression. Even with the hoodie obscuring his face, I knew who it was.

"Confession ended hours ago, sir," Jessica said, shutting her mahogany leather-bound notebook.

Archer glanced to his side before yanking the curtain open.

"Sir," Jessica repeated.

"You know what, it's okay." I stood, heading toward the booth. "I don't mind. Why don't you go home, I'll take care of this."

"Are you sure?" she asked hesitantly.

"Yes. I'll see you tomorrow?"

Jessica nodded. Once I was sure she was gone, I entered the

NINETEEN: THE PRIEST

booth.

Archer's cologne made my stomach flutter with excitement. The intensity of his gaze burned. Fearing he could see right through me, I broke eye contact and sat down. There was something about him that made me question everything I knew about myself.

"Father, I have sinned," he said.

I cleared my throat. "What has brought you here, my child?"

Archer chuckled, but surprised me by answering, "It's been a couple of weeks since my last confession—but you already know that," he said, leaning back with one hand in his pocket while the other rested on the back of the bench.

Memories of the night we shared came in droves, forcing me to look away. I'd never been fascinated by anyone the way I was by Archer. He wasn't the type of man I imagined when I pleasured myself. It wasn't often that I let weakness overtake me, but occasionally I did. I was a priest, not a saint, after all.

"What's the matter, Father?" Archer asked, eyes sparkling with mischief.

I grabbed the Bible resting on a small shelf, flipping the thin gilt pages with my shaky hands. I took a deep breath before reciting a verse I picked at random.

The sound of a belt buckle clanged, and when I looked at him, he was slowly undoing his belt, eyes still on mine. "What are you doing?" I asked, hoping that my voice wasn't as rattled as I felt inside. "This is the house of God."

"I can take you to heaven if you want ... again. Just say the word, Father," he said.

"What happened was a mistake," I whispered, on the off chance someone was lurking within earshot.

"You seemed to enjoy it, according to my recollection." He

bit his lower lip, winking.

"That's not the point. The point is it can't happen again."

"If you say so, Father."

I took a deep breath, exhaling slowly. "What brings you here?"

"To confess my sins."

"Let's hear it."

"Well." Archer rested his elbows on his knees, curving his back. He pulled his hoodie down, revealing a black eye. With the scar on his left side and his somewhat beat-up face, he exuded an air of danger and I couldn't get enough. "First, I fucked a priest, and I liked it," he growled.

I remained quiet, awaiting his next confession.

"And I killed another man," he added, appraising my reaction.

His second admission had my attention. *Again?* "Why did you kill him?"

He studied my face, his expression unreadable. "He was a monster."

"What does that make you?" I studied Archer's body language, determined to figure him out. "Are you the vigilante or the monster of your story?"

His calm expression morphed into something dark and gloomy. "He was a sad excuse for a man. Taking up air and space, so he had to go." Archer clenched his teeth, exaggerating his prominent jawline.

"What made you believe it was up to you to decide his fate? Only God can judge us." Anger betrayed our intentions, it weakened the mask and armor we wore, revealing truth in fury.

"I don't believe in God," he barked, looking away.

NINETEEN: THE PRIEST

That was a lie. I could tell when he broke eye contact. A small part of Archer's unveiling.

"Then why do you keep coming here?" I pressed. Archer sat, unaffected by my questioning, so I shared my opinion. "Let me tell you what I think."

"Enlighten me, Father." His hands balled into fists. If his looks were daggers, I would be dead. My brain screamed to be careful, but my gut urged me to keep pushing.

"You want absolution, Archer. You come here after you take someone's life thinking I can wash away your sins. You think you will be reborn when you step out of the four corners of this stall."

Archer gritted his teeth. "I'd be careful if I were you," he said, lifting the sweatshirt to expose his pistol tucked against his waist.

I ignored his bluff. "You think I'm your salvation. Am I getting close?"

"Fuck you," he said. "Fuck"—he pulled the gun from his pants and pointed it at me—"you." His agitation proved I'd been correct. "I can end you. Right here, right now."

"You could," I said, tucking my shaking hands into my pockets. "But you won't. Because I have a hunch—and I could be wrong—you only kill the bad guys. And I'm no bad guy."

"Don't fucking talk to me like you know me. You don't know shit about me." Archer's spit flung out of his mouth along with his rage.

"I can't save you. Only *you* can save you. So think about that when you storm out of here. Because you will." I looked at my watch. "In a minute."

"Fuck you and the golden high horse you ride on." As expected, he dashed out of the booth. The heavy wooden door slammed on his way out.

I blew out a shaky breath and withdrew my trembling hands. Provoking Archer wasn't smart, but it paid off. I hoped he was not the monster he claimed to be.

***

The door creaked open. Faint footsteps coming from the living room neared and I closed my eyes, pretending to be asleep. My heart raced as I listened to them approaching my bedroom. The movement halted, then the door opened. Thankful that my breathing was somewhat under control, I remained still, fearing that any action bigger than wiggling my pinky finger would give my ruse away.

The room filled with a familiar scent of citrus and mint, letting me know who had broken in. The scent became stronger as a shadow hovered over me. His breathing was heavy, and somewhat shaky when he exhaled. Surprising, since I hadn't pegged him as the nervous type.

A finger brushed my bare chest, soft like a butterfly. Ironic, considering he was anything but soft. His touch sent tremors to my core, an undeniable current of electricity coursed through me.

I shivered, causing him to stop. A sudden gloom of disappointment enveloped me when he shifted, perhaps to walk away. The urge to open my eyes was strong, but I kept them shut. I was about to sit up when the linen covering my body slid. The fabric dragged from my chest down to my abdomen. Painstakingly slowly, the silk sheet continued its journey down to my navel all the way to my obliques, where it stopped. My cock stirred, and my desire gathered to its length.

"Fuck," he whispered. The soft rustle from his careful movements made my heart pound. Then his palm, rough and hard, glided over the peaks and valleys of my abs.

I wanted so much to touch him, but it would give away my act. Keeping my hands to my sides, I remained motionless.

He pulled the cover further down, exposing all of me, the chilly air doing nothing to cool the burning fire between us.

Another deep and shaky breath cut through the deafening silence in the room. My mind, heart, and soul told me what I was doing was wrong on all levels. *What if people find out?* What my body desired defeated every rational thought. I would deal with the repercussions later, another weight to the sins I bore.

He was so still. I wondered if he was going to leave. I doubled down and spread my legs apart, hoping to draw his attention. I released a gasp when he grabbed my throbbing cock. The warmth of his touch hurtled me near the edge. I struggled to hold back the release threatening to erupt. I needed to last.

Twenty: The Reaper

He was awake, I was fucking sure of it. His eyes fluttered, the eyeballs following my every step through closed lids. Father Saint James gave up his last ace when he spread his legs apart. No way it wasn't intentional.

He was driving me fucking crazy. He must have had a death wish provoking me the way he did earlier. Only a mad man would do that. But, then again, he didn't have a clue who I was and what I was capable of. Storming out of the church was a needed separation between us. My instinct had been my north star guiding me through countless sticky and deadly situations, but not where he was concerned. I didn't know if my anger was toward him or me, for allowing someone like him to rattle me the way he did.

The priest shivered under my touch. I slid my palm up to the head of his dick, spreading the pre-cum leaking from the slit with my thumb.

He gasped.

Sleeping my ass.

If the father wanted to keep up this charade, I was fine with it. Having him lying naked on the bed, available to whatever I wanted, offered me a rare opportunity to explore his body.

It couldn't have been comfortable pretending to be sleeping with a rock-hard cock. What man alive hasn't woken up to find himself stiff and horny. So, if he wanted to play, I would willingly go along with his ruse.

While I rubbed my thumb across the head, I cupped his balls. His legs twitched and his cock flexed, the head expanding with each flex.

Spitting in my other hand, I brought them both to his cock and twisted up and down the shaft. Subtle cues of pleasure gave away how it must've felt for him, so I increased the friction and noticed his breathing had become ragged. I wondered if he thought he was having a wet dream. That was a possibility, but I still bet he knew exactly what was happening.

I kept the pace going as I twisted and tugged on his girthy piece. Moving a hand away, I gently moved it over his chest, cupping each pec as I crossed them and giving a soft twist to each nipple. Every time I pinched down on one, his cock sprung, letting me know the wiring was definitely connected.

I undid my jeans and shoved them down to my knees while keeping my attention on him and his burgeoning erection. He was leakier than a flat tire. Spreading his natural lubricant, plus my spit, each stroke became easier. My own cock was thickening and looked purple and angry from lack of attention. So, I rubbed, helping it achieve its full potential.

He remained quiet and motionless under my touch, so I leaned over him and took his cock in my mouth, licking around his mushroom head before slowly going all the way down on him until I felt him nudging my throat muscles. I had a mouthful, but I knew my way around a dick.

His cock was buried in my mouth and I tugged on his balls, massaging and squeezing them as I moved up and down on him. His breathing was heavy. He'd hold his breath with each tug on his balls until I relaxed the pressure and focused on his cock, then he'd slowly exhale.

My own dick was dripping and needed release bad, and since he was *sleeping*, I knew it would be up to me to find my own pleasure without any assistance from Sleeping Beauty. I stroked my cock, keeping time with the twist of my tongue around his dick. His breathing quickened and his legs stiffened straight out, locking his knees in place.

I deep-throated him and held his cock in place, feeling him swelling in my mouth. Very subtly he lifted his hips from the bed and met my mouth with small thrusts. I didn't care if he was awake, asleep, or in a fucking coma. His cock tasted amazing and I was down for whatever type of sex he wanted.

My orgasm was nearing and I carefully watched for hints that he was ready to bust a nut as well. My own breathing became heavier around his cock and I concentrated hard on pushing him over the edge. My speed and suction increased as he lifted his ass from the bed and forced into my throat as deep as he could. He'd remained careful not to move one of the hands lying by his side, even though I wished he'd grab the back of my head and face-fuck me. He seemed close, and so was I.

A gasp escaped his mouth one moment prior to him shooting his load into my mouth, and then he held his breath as I stayed focused on draining him completely. I enjoyed my mouthful of his cock and sucked gently until his tremors subsided. I smirked, sure he'd had a satisfying *dream*.

I stood, and when I thought he was done coming, his cock

shot another load onto his stomach.

Three pumps later, my own load gushed, coming all over Father Saint James's chest, some drops finding his cheek. I fought the desire to yell out loud from my enjoyment but stifled my moan.

I zipped my pants up once my breathing was steady. The sight of him covered with our releases was the most erotic scene I'd ever participated in, and I'd been involved in more than the average number of trysts. Fighting the urge to lick every drop of cum off his body, I pulled a small box from my pocket and dropped it on the nightstand. It was a golden rosary from Monaco, a gift for Father Saint James. I raised an eyebrow and glanced at the sleeping priest when I noticed the drawn curtains of his bedroom windows. Without hesitation, I pulled the drapes open before walking out.

I was next to my Harley when my phone buzzed in my pocket. A text from Tobias, The Savior. Finally. After a couple of weeks of radio silence, I'd dreaded something had happened to him. It wasn't far-fetched considering the lives we lived.

Same place at 11 PM tonight. I deleted the text, a precaution we took whenever we didn't want a trail of our conversations. I slid my phone back into my pocket without responding and whizzed through the quiet streets, the growling of my bike earning me a couple of looks from night crawlers like myself.

Going around my ass to get to my elbow, I spent an extra twenty minutes zipping through traffic and going out of my way to make sure I wasn't being followed. The parking garage for my apartment was quiet—almost too quiet. I carried my helmet in one hand while keeping the other on the gun at my waist. The sound of my boots pounding on the concrete floor echoed in the cavernous space.

The sound of rattling metal snatched my attention. I stopped. A loud bang slammed behind me. I drew my gun, whirling around.

"Damn car is dead," the guy said, kicking the front of his old beat-up Mustang. He glanced my way, eyes widening at the sight of me. He raised his shaking hands. "What the hell, bro? I ain't got no money 'n' shit!" he said, thinking I was there to rob him.

I wedged my gun back into my waistband after realizing it was my neighbor who'd caused the noise. Without an apology, I headed up to my floor. *I need to fucking calm down.*

I hadn't yet made it into my apartment when my phone buzzed with another text from Tobias.

Change of plans. Meet me @ Castle Island. Another message followed. *By the fort.*

I frowned at the screen. *Why? What's wrong?* I usually didn't text back, but this sudden change of plans had me feeling anxious.

Three bubbles appeared on the screen before his message appeared. *Tell you later.*

***

The crescent moon shone in the evening sky. The park was deserted since it was closed to the public after 7 p.m. Beneath the grove of mature maple trees stood a man in the shadows, scanning the premises. A light from his hand illuminated his face. My phone buzzed.

Tobias: *Is that you?*
Me: *Yeah.*
Tobias: *U weren't followed, were u?*

Me: *No.*
Tobias: *Follow me.*

Tobias waved and pointed to the concrete wall of the fort, urging me to follow him. I pulled my gun from its holster and made my way downhill after him. "Over here," he called from the third column.

"What happened?" I asked when I reached him.

His eyes bounced between the gun in my hand and my face. "Really?"

"I've been betrayed before," I said, tucking my gun back in.

"Fuck you," Tobias barked. "If you're not gonna trust me now, why the fuck should I put my life on the line for you?" He stared at me, waiting for an answer. "When will you realize that I'm on your side?"

It was wrong to make him feel that I didn't trust him, because I did. I never doubted he was on my side. It was my coping mechanism. After the deaths of Luke and William, I promised to never care for anyone, but I knew I had to with Tobias. It was only fair after what I'd asked him to do. "I'm sorry. I trust you," I whispered. As hard as it was to admit it, a sense of relief washed over me. "You know I hate last-minute changes," I added.

"You hate change, period."

I glared at him. "What happened to your face?"

His right eye was purple, while a small cut, held together by three stitches, highlighted his swollen cheeks. "Three men were waiting for me when I got home four days ago. They ransacked my place." He winced when lifting his arm to grab something from his coat.

"Goddamn it," I said, stepping closer to him. I lifted his shirt. My jaw tightened when I saw a patch of purple and blue skin covering his torso. "We can't do this anymore. I can't let you risk your life for me." I staggered back before turning toward my bike. If they wanted me, they'd need to come get me.

"Fuck that," Tobias said. He grabbed my elbow before I had the chance to walk away. "Listen to me, Archer. You're right. The Firm is involved in much shadier things than what you initially thought." He opened his jacket and pointed to an inner pocket.

I reached in and grabbed a stack of folded paper.

"They killed the senator because he was getting ready to expose them. Everything you need is on those pages."

I looked at the documents in my hand with relief. This was what I needed to take down The Firm and move on.

"They knew about you too."

I snapped my gaze to him. "What do you mean?" Nobody knew about my investigation except William. I hadn't even told him the whole story.

His expression darkened. "That's why they killed William."

"Fuck." I pulled my hair with both of my hands, pacing. How did they know?

"And that's why they came after me."

I shook my head in disbelief. "What happened to the guys who roughed you up?" I asked, pointing to his face.

"What do you think?" A dry laugh escaped his mouth, flinching as he held his battered side. "It's gonna take more than three rookies to take me down. They're looking for you."

"Let them look for me."

"How do you want to handle this now?" he asked.

"First, you need to get better."

"Then what?"

"We're going to expose every dirty deal they've done. I need that roster of their hits."

"Why?" Tobias asked, a knowing look on his face.

"Do you know Marilyn Ellis?" I'd been in communication with her about The Firm's wrongdoings, but she needed the proof before she aired her story.

"Yeah. How does she play in all this?"

"She'll expose them," I said. "But not without that list."

"Holy shit. There's no turning back from here, Archer."

I nodded. "I know. I won't blame you if you don't want anything to do with this. But I need to know. Are you in?"

I held my breath. Having Tobias, The Savior, on my side was essential. He was smart, strong, and more experienced than I was.

"Are you really attempting to take down one of the most powerful and influential groups in the United States?" he asked.

"They don't call me The Reaper for nothing."

"Let's fucking do this. We ain't got nothin' to lose."

If The Firm knew my plan of going rogue, it would only be a matter of time before they found me. They probably had someone coming to my place at that very moment. *Fuck!* So much for flying under the radar. I should've known. Their connections ran deep and wide.

I opted to spend the night in my new apartment and, as much as I hated to admit it, the dump was starting to grow on me. Besides, I planned on spending what little time I had left next to my priest. My obsession with him wasn't going away anytime soon, why fucking fight it? I was a dead man walking so I might as well enjoy my last meal.

Speaking of the devil. The lights in Father Saint James's room illuminated my computer screen. *What's he doing up this late?* It was two in the morning. A grin crossed my face when he rubbed his stomach and chest, the vision of my cock shooting my load over him made me want to rub another one out. But the smile on my face dissipated when a frown graced his handsome face, holding his cell closer to his ear.

Twenty-One: The Priest

"Is this Father Saint James?" a man with a thick accent asked.

A yawn escaped my mouth and I cleared my throat. "This is he," I croaked, glancing at my phone to check the time: 2:02 a.m. I groaned. My hand landed on my damp stomach, where the blend of our releases still pooled. Archer rutted on my *sleeping* body, making me feel like a cheap whore, and I loved every second of it. I pulled the phone away from my ear again. The caller ID was from overseas, the Vatican to be exact. That explained the hour of the call.

"Go to New Hampshire. Your presence is required in New Hampshire. The archbishop is waiting for you."

"When?" I asked, surprised at my ability to comprehend what was happening considering where my mind was.

"Wednesday at noon."

Wednesday? That was tomorrow. Actually in a few hours, since it was already after midnight. "I'm going to need longer notice than that," I reasoned while understanding the urgency of the matter. "How about in a couple of days? I will need to get a car."

"I'm sorry, Father Saint James, but that was the order. You

should have received an email about the meeting." He hung up before I had a chance to protest. It wouldn't make a difference anyway. Words were a waste of breath.

Since sleep was no longer an option, I headed to my office to check said email, stopping when a small white box caught my attention. Upon closer examination, the box was made from marble and was cool to the touch. Archer must've dropped this before he left a couple of hours ago. The thought of him made my skin burn with forbidden desire. I shook my head and placed it back on the nightstand, heading to the bathroom to clean up the evidence of my weakness.

While the coffee brewed, I tightened my robe and leaned against the marble counter. Fishing for my phone in my pocket, my fingers brushed against the USB drive. I stared at the offending piece of plastic and metal, feeling violated all over again. Frustrated, I tossed it on the counter and it bounced before sliding to a stop next to the knife block.

Glaring at it, I dug back into my pocket and retrieved my phone. After a couple of swipes, once I had entered a password, I stared at the encrypted email from the Vatican that was marked urgent.

Dearest Father Saint James,

I hope this email finds you well. We've received the memo of your relocation and below is the information for your meeting with our church leader in New Hampshire. They are expecting your presence on Wednesday, April 12, 2023, at 12:00 p.m. Accommodation for you has been arranged should you decide to stay overnight. This is an urgent matter and cannot be rescheduled. The success of your mission depends on this meeting. Time is of the essence.

Sincerely,
Archbishop Lloyd

TWENTY-ONE: THE PRIEST

While I was thankful that details about my mission were finally in motion, the seed of anxiety began to grow.

***

Hours later, my heart sank at seeing the flat tires on the car Jessica had rented for my trip to the Archbishop Retreat Mansion upcountry. "We can call for a replacement," she said, wringing her hands, her eyes red with tears and narrowed in confusion. "I don't know what happened. Tim and I drove it here just fine."

"It's okay." I tapped her shoulder, soothing her. "Abrupt change in weather does that sometimes." The temperature last night fell way below Boston's spring average, leaving frost on the ground. It could be why all four of the tires were flat. "We'll figure something out," I added. I needed to come up with a plan quickly if I wanted to make the noon meeting.

It'd been weeks since my arrival in Boston and I was desperate to learn more about my mission. Was I expected to stay here long term? Was there any special assignment? I glanced at my watch. I had exactly two hours to get there and, according to the map I saw early this morning, the driving distance to Sugar Hill would take a little over ninety minutes, and that was without traffic.

"Father?" Jessica asked, bringing me out of my musing.

"Yes?"

"Do you think you can reschedule to later today? I can call them and ask for a different car."

"Unfortunately, I can't reschedule." She wouldn't know that when they summoned you, you went.

The low purring of a motorcycle caused both of us to turn

toward the street. A sleek red bike stopped at the curb, the rider using a leg to balance. I couldn't see his face, but I knew who it was.

"I'll take you," growled the voice that stirred my desire.

Jessica gasped. "Who are you?" Her eyes were as big as dinner plates before they narrowed in suspicion.

"I'm a friend. Father Saint James and I go way back," he answered. Again, I didn't need to see the smug look on his face to know he was grinning beneath the tinted visor.

Jessica looked at me then back to Archer, who was now standing next to the rental car.

"What happened here?" he asked, examining the tires.

"Flat tires," I answered.

"Well, that's too bad," he said. He directed his attention to me. "I don't mind."

"I don't want to put you out because I need to stay overnight."

Jessica and the man stayed quiet. "So …" Jessica began. "You could at least get there, and Tim or I could pick you up tomorrow?"

This was the craziest idea ever, but I couldn't delay for much longer. "Okay," I said, picking up my small duffel bag from the ground. "Is there a place to store this?"

"We'll make it fit." Damn if that statement didn't make me feel hot and bothered.

"Let's go then," I said, and made my way to his motorcycle.

"Thank you," Jessica said, looking relieved that today hadn't turned out to be a disaster. "What's your name?" she asked, but Archer kept walking as if he didn't hear her question.

"Use this." He took his helmet off, handing it to me. He used his fingers to comb his wild hair back in place. He took his jacket off, revealing a tight black henley, and held it out as

TWENTY-ONE: THE PRIEST

well.

"No, I don't need that," I said.

"You'll freeze your ass off," he said. "This ain't no New Mexico."

"How did you know I was from New Mexico?"

He looked at me. "Seriously?"

I felt stupid. Anyone could google my name and find out that it was my last assignment. He grabbed my bag and placed it on top of a small platform, using bungee cords to secure it in place.

"What about you?" I asked.

He shrugged.

"What about a helmet? It's illegal to ride without one. Not to mention dangerous."

He looked at me before tapping my leg. "I have a smaller one," he said. He opened the small fiberglass compartment matching the color of his bike. "They have a microphone and small speaker so we can hear each other."

"Oh, okay," I said. I pulled the helmet over my head and was assaulted by citrus and mint. A wave of dizziness made my head spin as Archer's scent sent blood rushing south. This was going to be interesting.

He hopped on and pushed up the kickstand. "Ready?" he asked.

"Yeah." I climbed on behind him and stared at my hands. I looked at Jessica, who was watching us, and she waved. "Be careful, guys," she yelled.

"Wrap your arms around my waist," Archer ordered. I snaked my hands around his waist, feeling his hard stomach. I didn't know if it was my imagination, but I felt him shiver under my touch. "So, Father, where to?"

"New Hampshire," I answered. "And you can call me Heath since we're *friends* now."

"I can do that." Archer pulled my hands closer, tightening my hold on his body. "I still prefer Father though."

Twenty-Two: The Reaper

He looked like a man who would be named Heath. *Heath Saint James.* One of those fancy names belonging to an influential family.

"Are you ready?" I asked, basking in my brilliant plan. *I love it when shit goes accordingly.* I had stayed up watching for my priest, because his lights indicated he had been up all night. I might be a little selfish, but I wasn't about to let him go on a trip without me. I was just lucky that he didn't leave right away. Some quick pokes with an icepick and I was his savior.

Last night, while breaking into Father Saint James's home, I concluded it was my new favorite hobby. There was so much to him that was a mystery. Who was his late-night caller, why was he up before the break of dawn … my interest was piqued, so I paid him another visit. After he'd gone back to his bedroom, I crept into his office. The seat he'd vacated was still warm. I leaned back, picturing my back against his chest, his arms wrapped around me. A USB stuck out of one of the ports and I wondered about the content. *For another day,* I told myself, opening Father Saint James's email instead. The only email sitting in his inbox was an encrypted message from the Vatican.

"You didn't have anything to do with the flat tires, did you?" Heath asked.

Shit. Maybe my plan wasn't flawless after all. "Did you want me to have something to do with it?" I teased. He was a smart man; if he was asking the question, he already knew the answer. "I can sit here with you all day, if you have the time?"

"Let's go."

There was a first for everything, and having someone ride my motorcycle with me was something I never thought would happen, and I didn't know how I felt about it. Having Heath at such close proximity, his crotch pressing against my ass, should freak me the fuck out. I'd never been this close with anyone outside of fucking, and it was both scary and comforting.

Heath caressed my stomach with his thumb and I wondered if he was aware of the effect it had on my cock. A few more inches lower and he would realize just how much. We'd been on the road for thirty minutes and he was yet to say anything. Surprising, considering he usually had an onslaught of questions and assumptions.

"Sorry about yesterday," he said after another ten minutes.

"About what?" I asked, glad he couldn't see my knowing smile.

"I made an assumption and I was out of line. You came to confess and I should've kept it all about that. Instead of my own selfish agenda."

Well, that was unexpected. "What agenda?"

"It doesn't matter. It'd been a long day, and I have yet to have a full night's sleep since moving here. I'm exhausted." I knew that too, considering I was practically watching his every move since he arrived in Boston. "Say something," he demanded.

I wasn't much of a talker, but I could try. Another fucking first. "What do you want me to say?"

He blew out a breath. "Anything that's on your mind."

"Well, let's see …" I trailed off. A group of trained assassins are after me and want me dead because I'm the fucker who decided to dig shit up about their deals and connections, and then I called a network journalist to help expose The Firm. Oh, by the way, The Firm is an underground society of powerful men and women with links to the government and pretty much all industries in the US and other parts of the world. They were founded to right wrongs vigilante style, but started accepting money to kill almost anyone. Instead I said, "What are you gonna pay me for giving you a ride?"

"Oh, Jesus Christ," he grumbled. "I should've known."

"Never ask a question with an answer you're not ready for," I said.

"That's deep."

"That's me, all right. Deep."

"Do you prefer motorcycles over cars?" he asked after a prolonged silence.

"Yeah."

"What do you like about it?"

"It's liberating. Freeing." I didn't want to say more than that, I'd said too much already.

Cars slowed down, blue and red lights flashed half a mile ahead of us. My heart went into a frenzy, trying to jump out of my chest. The traffic stopped, but I kept moving, navigating through parked cars to get to the shoulder of the freeway.

"We should stop," Heath said.

"Nah, we're gonna be late." That was only one of the reasons.

I didn't trust that The Firm had nothing to do with what was going on up ahead. I didn't want to put the priest in danger.

I turned my handlebars to switch lanes, but a car jerked forward, blocking us. I banged on his car twice. The spot where my fist made contact left a dent on the hood.

The driver blasted his horn, raising his hands in the air.

I lifted my hand for another blow, but he backed up to allow us to pass. I flipped him off as a thank you.

"Calm down. I wanna get there alive."

"We'll be late," I said, revving the motor impatiently.

"We'll be okay." Heath rubbed my thighs, soothing the shit out of me. "Sorry about that," he yelled to the driver of the car.

"You're wasting your breath. He can't hear you," I said, tapping on my helmet. "I, however, can, and that fucking hurt my ears."

Four lanes and thirty seconds later, we were speeding ahead of everyone. The cops responding to the accident were too busy dealing with the flipped car and paid us no mind. I exhaled my relief.

***

"This is it," Heath said as we parked outside the gaudy black iron gate with alternating crosses and fleur-de-lis spikes plated in gold. A brick driveway separated two exceptionally well-manicured lawns that would make the groundskeeper of Wimbledon envious. A marble statue of Jesus Christ with cascading water from his hands decorated the middle of a roundabout. The two uniformed guards manning the ornate wooden doors had their narrowed gazes trained on us.

"Subtle design," I said.

TWENTY-TWO: THE REAPER

Heath laughed before removing his helmet. "Here," he said, handing it back to me. "Thanks again. Since I might stay the night, you don't have to wait." He loosened the cord tied around his bag. "Be safe going back."

"How are you gonna get home?" I asked, ignoring the disappointment gnawing inside my rotten core.

"I'll figure it out." He turned but I grabbed his hand before he took his first step. He looked down at our joined hands in surprise.

"Fuck that." I pulled my cell from my pocket. "I'm taking you home. What's your number?"

"Archer, don't—"

"Number," I demanded.

"Okay, okay." I tapped each digit as he spoke them, then pressed the call button.

He raised an eyebrow as he grabbed the vibrating phone from the pocket of his bag. "What are you doing?" Heath showed me his caller ID with my number.

"Just making sure you didn't give me the wrong number," I said. It wasn't one of my proudest moments. "I'll find an Airbnb for tonight. Call me when you're ready."

"If you insist." He walked toward the gate, pressing a button beside a speaker. "My name is Heath Saint James. I have an appointment at noon."

"Welcome, Father. I'll buzz you in," a crackly voice said through the speaker.

I turned the ignition but stopped when Heath called out.

"What about your jacket?" he asked, unzipping my leather jacket.

"Keep it. I'll get it later."

The gate opened and Heath waved goodbye before he

entered the mansion.

***

After entering the code to the rustic tiny home I'd booked from Airbnb, my watch lit up announcing a phone call from El Jefe. I ignored it and made my way inside. Online images of this place were deceiving; it was way smaller inside. My tour consisted of a ninety-degree turn, and I could touch the ceiling when I raised my hand. But it had a private bed and bathroom, so it would do.

"Go away," I said when El Jefe's name flashed on the screen again, then again, then again. I didn't want another assignment, I needed time to get that list. This time a voice mail followed. Finally, a text.

Call me ASAP, it read.

Newsflash: I didn't. I was seconds from shutting my phone off when Zero's name flashed. She never called. My curiosity got the best of me and I accepted her call. "What's up, Zero?"

"Hey, bro! Are you in some kind of trouble?"

My heart jumped out of my chest at her question. Did she know something I didn't? I took a deep breath to calm the tension building in my neck and shoulders. The knots in my stomach were back with a vengeance. "Aren't we always in trouble?" I asked, sounding like my typical not-a-care-in-the-world attitude.

"That's a fact."

"Why did you call?" I asked

"El Jefe asked me to track your phone," she said between the loud clicking of her keyboard.

What the fuck? "Did you tell him?" Why did he want to

know where I was? Was he the one who'd outed my plan? That couldn't be it, could it? Paranoia had planted a seed in my head. The circle of people I trusted was shrinking as my world was collapsing.

"Not yet. I'm on an assignment right now and will do it later."

Good. "Give me an hour and tell him my phone was left at my apartment where you tracked it to."

"Are you in your apartment? Don't even try lying. You know I'll be able to tell."

I knew that. "Not right now, but I will be in an hour." Now that I didn't have to worry about Father Saint James's safety, I could shave time to get back home.

"You better be there when I track you. K, gotta go."

I broke several traffic laws on my way back to Boston. When I reached the city limits, I glanced at my watch, groaning because I had ten minutes before Zero ran the location of my phone. I twisted the throttle, accelerating dangerously and zigzagging between the crawling cars.

My legs burned and felt like jello after I ran up eight flights of steps to my apartment. When my breathing was somewhat under control, I grabbed the extra burner phone I kept and entered three sets of numbers to my contacts: Heath, Tobias, and Zero.

Me: *Hey Heath, this is Archer. Use this number instead.*

Me: *Hey Tobias! El Jefe might be onto me. Don't send anything. Just call this number if you find anything.*

Tobias: *Fuck! Are you sure?*

Me: *Not really. Tell you more later.*

Tobias: *Stay alive.*

Me: *That's the plan.*

It wasn't safe there anymore. I grabbed a bag from my closet and crammed it with extra guns, ammo, clothes, and stacks of hundred-dollar bills. After tossing my phone and the watch into the wooden bowl on the counter, I bailed.

Twenty-Three: The Priest

My hands were clammy and my whole body was sweating while I waited in the receiving hall of the archbishop's mansion. I'd been waiting for almost two hours and had yet to be brought inside the office. Why would they have me come in early if they planned on keeping me waiting? I pulled Archer's leather jacket off to prevent myself from overheating. This was ridiculous. I wasn't here to be reprimanded but to discuss my mission. Nothing more, nothing less. I stood, fanning my face with my hand. *Breathe, Heath. You'll be fine. They don't know what you've done.*

The ride with Archer momentarily distracted me from obsessing over this meeting. It'd been the most fun I'd had in years.

My phone pinged with a text notification from a number I didn't recognize. *Hey Heath, this is Archer. Use this number instead*. What happened to his phone? I was getting ready to respond when the door opened.

A man wearing a black cassock headed in my direction. "Father Saint James?"

"Yes."

"The archbishop is ready for you," he said. "Follow me,

please."

I grabbed my bag, sliding Archer's jacket between the loops.

"How was your trip?" he asked, glancing over his shoulder.

"It was fine. It was a miracle I made it here on time considering the short notice." It was meant as a joke, but I was still bitter about the entire ordeal. What if Archer hadn't been around? Would they have come to see me instead? I doubted it.

"You know the Church. Everything is urgent," he said.

"That I know very well."

He ushered me inside another waiting area, this one with a door guarded by two men. "Wait here," he said before disappearing behind the guarded door.

Awkwardly, I stood in the middle of the room. Remembering to send a quick text to Archer, I typed *Sounds good* before silencing my phone.

The door opened moments later. "They're ready," the man announced.

Narrowing my eyes, I stepped forward. "They?" I asked when I reached him.

"Yes." He gestured for me to enter the room, closing the door firmly behind me.

I was greeted by three leaders of the Church when I entered the stuffy office. The walls were covered with oil paintings depicting the teachings of Jesus Christ. The purple velvet curtains were drawn closed, with only two lampshades illuminating the dim room. In front of a framed map of the Old World was Archbishop Lloyd, who was wearing a white alb finished with a red and gold chasuble. Two other priests in the same regalia sat on either side of him.

"Please," Archbishop Lloyd said, motioning to the chair

TWENTY-THREE: THE PRIEST

across from him.

"Thank you," I said. I sat and kept my hands under the polished wooden table. I noted that I was sitting by myself and tried to ignore the intimidation.

"Has Andrew contacted you?" one of the men asked.

I thought about how to answer the question. I received a phone call from his number, but that was the extent of my communication with him. "No, I haven't spoken to Andrew," I answered. "I'm sorry, we haven't met …?" I asked, my eyes bouncing between the two unfamiliar men.

"I'd like you to meet Cardinals Lopez and O'Brien," the archbishop said.

"Pleased to meet you."

They responded with a nod, glancing at the archbishop in synchrony.

"Have you heard from him?" I asked, assuming Andrew would've tried to reach them too.

"No communication from him recently." Archbishop Lloyd slid a tablet across the table, the subject of Andrew apparently dropped. "Details of your mission."

I tapped the screen to life and brought it closer to my face when it asked for facial recognition. A single folder named *Boston Project* was on the home screen. I scrolled through the file, keeping a neutral face, taking steady breaths. My hands trembled when an image of Archer and I standing an inch apart, Archer's tongue about to lick my earlobe and my face flush with barely disguised lust, stared back at me.

Oh no. Oh no no no no no …

I recalled the moment with clarity. It was the Sunday after my first mass, when Archer had propositioned me and those tourists had interrupted us.

I dropped the tablet on the desk, shooting them a look. They knew about me and Archer. "How did you—"

"It doesn't matter how. We still believe you're the right man for the mission," Cardinal Lopez said before I had a chance to finish my question.

"But … won't this complicate things?" Was I the only one who thought this mission was already compromised? My face burned, and I shifted my glance down to the polished table. I couldn't bear to look them in the eyes, but I could still see their reflections.

"Only if you let it." It was Cardinal O'Brien's turn to speak this time.

"I have one word." Archbishop Lloyd rested his joined hands on the table. "Discretion."

One word. That was the last word they uttered before I was ushered out of the office. I felt like a fool. They had known all along.

"Can you point me to the nearest restroom?" I asked my escort, the same man as before. "I better go before I hit the road again."

He hesitated for a second, but pointed to the end of the hallway. "To your left," he said. "I'll wait for you by the main entrance."

I released a shaky breath when I entered the marbled bathroom, heading to the sink to splash cold water on my face. I stared at my dripping reflection. "You can do this," I told myself. One last mission, then I would reconsider what I wanted to do for the rest of my life.

I didn't realize how long I was in there until a soft knock caught my attention. The door opened and the man peeked inside. "You have to go," he said.

TWENTY-THREE: THE PRIEST

"Give me a minute," I said, fishing my phone out. "I have to text my ride."

He shook his head, rolling his eyes. "Okay."

I opened Archer's message to let him know about the change of plan.

Me: *I'm going to have Jessica pick me up today. Thanks for the offer.*

I wasn't sure why it made a difference, since the Church knew about Archer. The archbishop's voice replayed in my head. *Discretion.*

Archer: *Fuck no. I'll be there in a minute.*

Me: *In a minute? Where r u?*

The door opened and Mr. Impatient walked in. "You really need to get going," he stressed.

"Understood," I said, and left.

A couple of priests were walking toward us as we made our way to the lobby. They smiled and I nodded in acknowledgment. I didn't know them personally, but I'd seen them in one of the meetings organized by the Church. Their escort led them to the waiting room I'd been in just minutes ago.

The metal gate clicked, locking me out the moment I stepped off the property. Shaking my head, I looked behind me and sighed. My phone rang.

"Look to your right," Archer said when I answered. He was standing next to his bike, a block away from the mansion. He was wearing a dark helmet and I couldn't see his face. "Ready to go?"

"Yeah," I said. "I'll come over there." I didn't want anyone to see me taking off with him.

Archer handed me the same helmet I'd used earlier. "I thought you were spending the night?"

"Are you kidding me? They couldn't wait to get me out of there." I wouldn't have stayed even if they had offered.

"Let's go then." We hopped on his bike. Archer grabbed my trembling hand, scorching my skin with his touch. I wrapped them around his waist. "Ready?" His hand dangled to his side, squeezing my leg.

"Yes," I said, tapping his stomach.

Wind swept over my body, the chill causing me to shiver. I'd been in such a state of disbelief that I'd forgotten to put on his jacket. I pressed my chest closer to Archer's back for warmth, hoping he wouldn't notice.

"You should've worn the jacket," he said.

"I'm okay," I lied.

"No, you're not. You can put it on when we stop by the Airbnb."

We hit a bump, causing my grip on his waist to tighten. "You actually rented a place for the night?"

Archer shrugged.

"Why?"

"I wanted to take you back to Boston." He turned onto a wooded driveway, stopping by a tiny rustic home next to a pond. Its deck hung over the water, a small row boat tied to it.

"Wow. It's beautiful out here." Mature pine trees hid this gem from the main road. I stretched my arms over my head, enjoying the sounds of birds singing and the rustling of trees.

He was studying me when I opened my eyes. He raked my body with his gaze, swallowing when it came back to my face. "I'm gonna go get my stuff," he said.

"Wait," I called.

He turned but remained quiet.

"I wanna see the inside."

TWENTY-THREE: THE PRIEST

"Okay," he said. He went ahead and unlocked the door.

Archer was standing at the other end of the room by the time I made it inside. He was definitely putting space between us, and I didn't know how I felt about that. He'd been quiet as well, and that was saying something, since he was a man of very few words.

"It's cozy," I said, looking around the small space as I walked toward the bed. I ran my fingers over the plush comforter before sitting down. "You should stay the night. It'd be nice to get out of the city and recharge."

He shrugged, walking closer, stopping by the door. "I made a promise to drop you off, so I can't stay."

"Who cares? They're just words, and we barely know each other. You should stay since you already paid. I can get a ride."

"My words mean everything to me." Archer looked out the window, but I doubted he was seeing the beautiful scenery in front of him. "I mean what I say and I say what I mean. Without my word, I really am nobody."

I thought about his words and the deeper meaning behind them. Before I could overthink it, I blurted, "Let's stay." What was another night? My superiors knew about me and him, so why not have the best night before this was over?

He snapped his head to me, raising his eyebrow. "Do you think you'll be safe here? Alone with me?" he asked. The mischief in his eyes was back.

"Maybe you're the one in danger," I answered.

Archer stepped into the room and turned to shut the door. He leaned his head against the wood frame and I saw his shoulders rise when he inhaled. "Get naked," he ordered, before turning to face me with narrowed eyes full of lust.

I stood with the intention of removing my clothing one item

at a time. Starting with my shirt, I unbuttoned it from the top, slowly releasing each button, before letting the soft material slide down my arms. I yanked my undershirt over my head in one swift movement, then tossed it at Archer's feet. He watched it land in front of him before returning his gaze to me, licking his lips before an audible swallow. My shoes and socks were next. I sidestepped and turned so that my back was to him before I bent over and shimmied out of each shoe. Once my socks were off, I stood and loosened my belt before pulling it slowly through the loops. I faced him again then proceeded to unbutton my pants, letting them fall to the floor. I stepped out of them one leg at a time.

"Take everything off," he growled, glaring at my boxers.

I hooked my thumbs in my waistband, dragging them down to my feet. When I stood, I was naked.

Archer leaned against the wall, taking in my body from head to toe. "Play with yourself," he ordered. His voice was husky and deep; every word sounded like a growl. Feral and aroused.

My hazy, lust-induced brain took a moment to reconcile what was happening. And before I second-guessed my action, I dragged my tongue over my right palm first, then the left, never breaking eye contact.

He swallowed hard when I double-fisted my cock.

"Like this?" I asked. The sound of my voice was foreign to me.

"Just like that, baby." He rushed forward then, pushing me onto the bed. Archer straddled me as he pulled his shirt over his head to reveal his chiseled torso. "Just like that."

Twenty-Four: The Reaper

I couldn't seem to get away from Heath. I was willing to put everything behind and focus on what I needed to do, but, like a junkie, he was my vice. His offer came as a surprise, but I would be lying if I said I didn't crave him. Scratch that. I didn't crave it, I fucking loved it.

The call from Zero had been the wakeup call I needed to snap me out of the pull he had on me. If El Jefe was aware of my ploy and was about to send someone to hunt me, then I was running out of time. The plan was to drop off the priest at his house, as promised, then meet Tobias to figure out a way to oust The Firm without the list.

But that came crashing down the moment Heath offered to stay.

Heath wiggled his body beneath me, his hands going for my nipples, but I grabbed both of them and pinned them over his head. "You think you would've learned from the last time," I said, transferring my weight onto his stomach.

He thrust his hips up to throw off my balance, causing the mattress springs to squeak. "I can take you down," he said before rolling to his side.

"Fuck!" I cursed. I was outmaneuvered when he rolled us to

the floor. I didn't expect to be dragged with him. The entire house shook from our weight, and I thought for a second the tiny building might break.

A boisterous laugh escaped his lips. His mouth was wide open, his eyes were glistening with joy, catching the light from outside. He was … beautiful. His laugh and the sparkle in his eyes eased my worries and alarmed my psyche. It wasn't that I didn't like it. No, it was because I loved it a little more than I should.

He jabbed my side, and I winced before grabbing his hands again. Instead of pinning them over his head, I restrained them to his sides. He squirmed, but that was the extent of what he could do. I had him where I wanted him.

"Out of moves?" I asked.

A menacing smirk graced his handsome face before he lifted both of his legs, locking my upper body with them. He twisted until my back slammed against the wall. "You're fucking strong," I said, turning my back against him. With all my force, I used my legs and arms to push my body up until we were both standing.

I rammed his body against the door. His lips were inches away from mine, our chests touching when we filled our lungs. He stared at my lips, then my eyes. Darting his tongue out to wet his lips was a soundless invitation.

I wanted to kiss him. It was the first time I'd ever felt the urge to kiss someone. Alarm bells rang in my head, warning me a kiss was a terrible idea. But, just like his offer to stay, I was weak when it came to his invitations. I leaned closer, his breath fanning my lips. Our eyes locked, his pull on me strengthening. I closed the sliver of distance between us.

Heath's lips parted and I didn't hesitate to dive in. We

explored each other's mouths with our tongues, sucking, nipping, licking, only parting to gasp necessary air. He moaned and lifted his hands to caress my chest. His hands traveled to my neck, pulling me closer.

I wrapped my arm around his waist. I needed to be as close as possible to him, an impulse bordering on obsession. We were skin on skin, but somehow it wasn't enough. I wanted him to smell like me hours after we'd parted. I bit the skin on his shoulder, firm enough to leave marks but not hard enough for his skin to break.

Heath's body turned rigid before he shoved me away, panting. He glanced to his side where the bite mark was, then back at me. His eyes were flaming with desire. He smirked before yanking my head so our mouths collided. The force caused a faint salty, metallic taste to linger before the kiss turned tender and sweet.

Wait, I didn't do anything tender and sweet. I pulled away and glared at him.

I wanted it rough and harsh.

My encounters had always been one-sided, with me in control and often not returning the favor. The people I'd fucked and let suck me off were tools for my pleasure, and I didn't give a rat's ass about them.

What was it about this priest? Even if I tried to convince my mind to disengage, my physical self couldn't do it. He pressed his body harder against mine, and our mouths collided again, teeth gnashing and hands pulling at one another. His strength was a little intimidating. I wasn't used to a sexual partner that exhibited vigor and toughness the way he did. The man hidden in the cloak of religion was not the man currently attached to my lips.

Heath wrapped his arms around my neck then leapt up and wrapped his legs around my waist. I held him against the wall and we continued smothering each other's breaths with passionate and fiery kisses.

Passion.

I shook my head and pulled away to stare at him. Men like me didn't get to experience passion. Emotion was a cancer, budding from a speck into annihilation.

We were fucking. Anything other than lust wasn't welcome.

He searched my eyes then moved his mouth to my ear. "Fuck me, Archer," he breathed against the sensitive skin. "I need you in me right now."

I carried him to the bed and he fell backward, but I had other ideas in mind. I bent over and grabbed his legs, twisting them until he flopped onto his stomach.

"Scoot up," I demanded, reaching for my bag by the side of the bed.

I fished lube and a foot-long strip of foil packs from it. I tore the wrapper with my teeth and used my tongue to pull the rubber from it while I stroked my cock with lube. Heath tried rolling to his side but I brought my foot up to his back and shoved him flat onto the bed again, the mattress squeaking in protest.

"Face down and stay still," I barked.

I crawled over him and rested my weight on him, biting into his neck as my cock slid between his butt cheeks and I pumped into the space between his legs.

"Yeah," he moaned into the mattress.

"Spread your cheeks, Father," I said. "Let me see that fuck hole."

I adjusted to all fours and slid back so I could focus on his ass after he held them apart with his hands.

"Like that?" he asked.

My hand came to his hole with a smear. One finger slid in and I let him engulf it before retreating then sending two in next. He relaxed around my digits, so I added a third and shoved them deep. He gasped but met me with an eager acceptance.

"Hold them apart," I ordered, moving above him again and aligning my cock to his ass cheeks. He held them apart while I slapped his pucker with my dick, teasing and warning him. I pushed in fully with one thrust. He tried to squirm from under me, but I had my knees on either side of his legs, giving him nowhere to go.

"Shit," he cursed, still straining under me. "A little warning next time?"

"You'd be lucky if there's a next time, so fuck off and shut up."

There couldn't be a next time.

I pumped into Heath, pounding him into the mattress as he groaned under my weight. He arched his ass up and met me with equal enthusiasm, so I buried the length of my cock as deep as I could and held it there before pulling out and slamming back into him.

"That's it," he exhaled when I pressed against his prostate with every punch of my cock. "You're hitting it," he added. "Harder!"

I changed position and kneeled between his legs, shoving them apart with brute strength and exposing his ass to me. Once again I buried deep and held my cock in him, but this time I leaned forward, grabbed a fistful of his hair, and held his face into the mattress while I fucked him aggressively.

"What about now? This enough for you?"

He didn't answer. Or couldn't answer, I wasn't sure and didn't give a fuck either way. His muffled moaning was all I heard coming from a mouth being forced to eat the mattress. I let go of his head. I gripped his hips and yanked his ass up in the air so he was on his knees. His back arched with his head still against the mattress, but I elbowed him to make sure his face stayed down.

Heath had a round and meaty ass. Each cheek a perfect half-volleyball-sized mound of smooth and muscular flesh. His asshole was stretched around my dick. I loved watching my cock go in and out of him, staking my claim. I leaned forward and grabbed a handful of hair, pulling his head back like a show pony while bearing down on his sweet asshole.

"That's it," he yelled. "Just like that."

His hips ground, meeting my thrust with urgency. I slapped his ass hard enough to leave a red mark, the only blemish on an otherwise perfect sculpture.

"You like that, bitch?" I asked, letting go of his hair. I moved both of my hands around his neck, choking him from behind and pulling him so hard backward that his hands left the mattress. "What about this?"

His hands came behind and held his ass cheeks apart as far as he could. He might be barely breathing, but the answer was clear: he wanted this, he needed more of what I was serving.

I flipped him over, giving him momentary relief, and pinned him to the bed by straddling his chest. His dick was solid and leaking like a faucet. This man loved sex and had an affinity for the kind I craved: rough and rowdy. Who fucking knew?

His hands were pinned to his sides by my legs as I sat on his rib cage, but he still wore a shit-eating grin. I leaned over him and let saliva drip from my mouth onto his, using my hands to pinch his cheeks and force it open.

"More?" I asked.

He glared at me while I held his mouth in my hand, his eyes laser focused on mine. Whatever he was feeling, fear sure as fuck wasn't it. He didn't speak but his eyes told me everything.

I moved to my knees and slid down to his thighs where I lifted his legs. Once I locked the inside of my elbows behind his knees, I leaned forward, bringing his legs with me until his knees nearly touched his ears. He was fully exposed.

Our eyes locked again. He still hadn't spoken a word. I hoped he was focused on going along for the ride and giving himself over to me completely. I wanted him to *want* to be owned by me. I could do that. I would do that.

My cock pressed around his ass while I remained above him, moving my hips until I positioned it on his entrance. Once there, I reentered him with one slow stroke until my hips pressed against his thighs. This new position enabled me to ram into him deeper.

"Oh my god!" he screamed. His hands gripped my shoulders and he held me tightly as I moved in and out, meeting him halfway as we moved in unison. He'd pulled my head to the side of his while holding me so close we'd become one. My hands instinctively went behind his head and I cradled him closer while we exhausted our bodies in a wild fraught ritual.

"Take me, Archer," he gasped into my ear. "Take me all the way."

I was down for the invitation, whichever way it was intended. I moved my head from the side of his and captured his lips with my own hungry mouth. At first our kissing was violent, angry, needy, and born of inflicted pain, but slowly it morphed as our bodies became one, one motion of satisfaction.

I was inside Heath, and he willed me to stay there in a kind of dance I didn't understand. But in that moment, it didn't matter, because an overwhelming desire to fulfill a needed gratification had taken us both over.

Heath's hands slid to my ass cheeks and he pulled me into him harder, challenging me to keep up the pace.

"Right there," he moaned. "Oh yes, Archer. Right there!"

His head rolled back and his pupils disappeared, only the whites of his eyes visible. Whatever was happening to him came on so fast that at first I was concerned I was killing him, but the moans of pleasure convinced me otherwise.

The more he moaned and begged me to keep hitting that sweet spot, the hotter it got. My pace quickened while I studied an animalistic look I'd never seen. He was obviously seeing red while giving a green light, so who was I to deny him?

"I'm gonna shoot," I hissed. "Fuck!"

"Not yet! Not yet!"

His cock was rubbing against my stomach as he lifted his hips toward me, holding on for dear life. He planned to fuck his own load out and he was gonna use my cock buried in his ass to get there. My idea was the same as his. The more he moaned and ground against me, the more my aggression increased to match.

"Yes!" he yelled. "Oh god! Oh god!" He bucked hard under me until his body stiffened, blasting his release between us. His head fell back and he panted like a dog.

I had my cock sheathed deep when his body clamped around me, snatching my soul through my balls and into him. I didn't recognize the growl that vibrated through my chest.

I collapsed onto him and we stayed like that for what seemed like forever.

We went for a second round, and then a third, only resting to replace the condom. My balls were dry after the fourth round, and after hours of fucking, I was spent, and if Heath's sexed-out eyes and extremities spread out on the floor was an indication, it appeared he was too. I reached for a pillow and lifted Heath's head onto it.

"Thanks," he whispered.

I lay on my side, nestling my face on my bent arms. "Your skin is so smooth." I dragged the back of my hands up and down over his abdomen.

He chuckled, but he didn't look at me. His attention was directed outside, where the sun was setting behind the stand of pine trees surrounding us.

I reached for his messy hair, combing it to the side where his natural part was, allowing myself to be tender for once. What did I have to lose? This would be over soon.

"After today, I won't bother you anymore," I said. A sense of dread hit my core. This must be how it felt when people quit their addictions cold turkey. "I'll drop you off and I'll be out of your life forever."

Heath shifted and mirrored my position, facing me. His brows furrowed, confusion in his eyes. He didn't think we would keep this up forever, did he? "What do you mean?"

"I'm bored. Time to move on," I lied.

He shook his head. "I'm not buying that. Whatever happened to say what you mean and mean what you say?" The asshole was using my words against me. "Tell me the truth and I promise to keep it with me."

I studied him, debating whether I should.

"Just like confessing your sins," he added.

I shook my head before rising to my feet. I reached for my jeans, pulling them on before heading outside. I could not get him involved.

Everyone you touch turns up dead, the voice in my head said.

"I'm sparing you," I murmured to the wilderness.

Hours passed. He must've known I needed the space. The moon and stars reflecting off the pond kept me company. I banged my head with my fists, frustration building inside me. I wanted my edge back; being with Heath had disarmed me. He was a fucking priest, for fuck's sake. There was no way this would end well, even in the best of circumstances.

Shuffling came from behind me, followed by footsteps and the smell that was forever etched in my mind.

"You must be cold." Heath wrapped a warm blanket around my freezing body. He sat next to me, his hands resting on his knees. "How did you get this?" he asked, caressing the scar above my eye.

I'd never told anyone. I wanted to tell him, but doing so would reveal a part of me that was long gone.

"Tell me," he urged.

Twenty-Five: The Priest

"I can tell you, but I'd have to kill you," he said, not looking at me.

His face was cold under my touch. I'd let him be after he walked out, and dusk had turned to chilly night. I'd spent those hours reading the details of my mission, studying everything I'd been given for success, the redemption I came here for. This was my chance to prove I wasn't a complete failure and waste of time.

And it was … not what I imagined it would be. At all.

I'd noticed Archer's gun on the counter of the tiny kitchenette, and I felt an urge to hold it, feel the weight of cold metal in my hand. I turned it over, examining it, and wondered how many people had fallen at the hands of its owner. It was then I looked out the window and found him sitting on a patch of grass near the pond. His head was tucked between his legs; the moonlight made his exposed back glow. I grabbed the blanket draped over the small armchair before heading outside.

I wasn't sure why I was pushing him to open up so much. He was right with what he'd said earlier: it was time for him to go. Whatever we were doing, it couldn't continue. Maybe that was why I pushed, so I would remember him when he was gone. He wasn't always what he appeared to be on the surface. We all have a facade we hide behind. I was a great example of that. I was a priest with a secret more lethal than the people Archer had confessed to killing.

"I didn't want this life," I admitted, offering something about myself. *Trust begets trust.* His head shifted, peeking to meet my gaze. Archer remained silent, so I kept going. "I never wanted to be a priest." I shook my head.

"Then why did you choose it?" he asked. "Why did you go through all the bullshit to be a priest if it's something you didn't want?" He lifted his head, watching me closely.

"I came from a family of priests. My uncles were priests, and so is my brother. I didn't have a choice."

"That's the stupidest thing I've ever heard. How can you not have a choice?" The crease on the sides of his eyes deepened. "You're an adult. You can make your own decisions."

"You don't understand. I wish it was that easy."

Archer eyed me, his gaze intensifying. He rubbed his chin, now covered with a blond five o'clock shadow. He leaned forward, pausing when we were face-to-face. His eyes were filled with hesitation. He stared at my lips, swallowing. The arrogant persona he used as a default faltered when he released a shaky breath. Something dark was brewing inside him, and I was ready for his storm. "Do you really want to know?"

I nodded. "Tell me."

"I shouldn't," he whispered. He combed his hair with his fingers before dragging them down to his face and neck.

"Shouldn't or won't?" I pressed, wondering about the possible reasons that could hold him back. "You can tell me anything."

Another deep breath escaped Archer's pursed lips. He closed

TWENTY-FIVE: THE PRIEST

his eyes, his jaw tightening, and I couldn't help but feel sorry for him. The turmoil he was fighting must've been so great that the idea of sharing it with someone caused him distress. "I got it when I was younger. Eighteen, maybe nineteen." He ran his finger over the scar. "I was sentenced to life for the murder of four of my classmates, including my only friend, Luke." He pinched the bridge of his nose. "God, Luke," he whispered.

My eyes widened, and he must've witnessed my shock because he shook his head repeatedly. I remained silent and focused on every word coming from his mouth.

"I didn't do it. I was framed." His eyes begged me to trust him. "You have to believe me."

"I do believe you," I said. I'd only known him for a short time, but my gut was telling me to trust him. *I mean what I say and say what I mean.* I repeated his mantra in my head.

"I was so afraid. You should've seen my grandparents. They were devastated." Archer looked up at the sky, his watery eyes shining.

"Did they believe you were innocent?"

"They did. They raised me, after all," he said. "I was a good kid. I did well in school and stayed out of trouble. Even still, I ended up in prison."

"What about your parents?"

He shook his head. "Mom told me my dad was killed in the Gulf War. Then she disappeared when I was eight years old. My grandparents spent so much money looking for her, even hiring several private investigators. But after ten years, they gave up. All efforts were a waste of time."

"I'm sorry. That must've been awful." I rubbed his back, my heart breaking for him. I knew too well how that felt. I'd lost my parents at an early age too.

"They visited me in prison every week without fail. They attended my trial, which lasted for almost a year. Do you know how hard it is to witness someone you love die inside? The ugly truth of losing me dulled the light in their eyes, but they kept fighting until the end." A stray tear fell on his cheek, and he quickly wiped it away.

"I do know," I admitted. "I know how ugly the world can be."

"You don't have to say that. What would you know? You have this perfect, holier-than-thou world."

"I'm just like you," I said.

"No, you're not. You wouldn't know ugly if it hit you in the face," Archer whispered. "The unimaginable ugliness looming outside the sanctuary that has sheltered you."

His assumptions were as unfair as my own back in the confessional. But I understood. "I know more than you think I do." I wanted to scream, but couldn't. I wouldn't. Emotion was a liability.

"You don't know pain." He gritted his teeth, pointing his finger at me. "The kind of pain that extinguishes hope and destroys any shred of happiness because it's dangerous to feel anything at all."

Archer was an enigma, beauty within chaos. Another wave of silence passed and I feared that he'd finished spilling his truth, so I bit the bullet and asked, "What happened next?"

To my surprise, Archer continued.

"The day I was taken to the state penitentiary, the bus escorting me was ambushed by two vans blocking the road. Everything happened so fast, it's all a blur. I just remember a huge explosion and then hanging upside down, dangling from my seat with my cuffs digging into my wrists." Archer rubbed his thumb over a scar on his wrist before covering his eyes with his fists, his muscles flexing at the force.

"Hey, it's okay." I pulled his hand away from his face and forced him to look at me.

"Waking up in a bright room was the next thing I remember. My left eye was covered with gauze and I thought I'd lost it."

"Were you in hospital?"

Archer shook his head. "I found out later it was some facility belonging to ..." He paused, looking unsure. After a couple of seconds, he continued. "The Firm."

I held my breath, hoping he would keep going. I didn't want to say anything, fearing it would stop him from revealing more.

"That's how I met this guy Carlos. Everyone in The Firm calls him El Jefe, because he is our leader. He was more than my leader. He was like a father."

"What about the authorities? Are they still looking for you?"

"The Firm faked my death. They gave me a new identity. Many identities, actually." A dry laugh escaped his lips. "John Smith, Peter Robinson, Roy Green. I can be anyone I want, as long as it isn't the real me. They told me never to contact my grandparents because of the consequences. And I learned recently that the only consequence is death."

"Wow." I exhaled. "Your poor grandparents." I had to know more about his participation with this group. "What do you do for The Firm?"

Archer cautiously appraised me but spoke anyway. "I belong to an underground society of assassins and mercenaries run by an elite group called The Firm. We are capable of wiping an entire community out in one night. We were ..." He stopped talking, glancing round. He became fidgety.

"No one is here but us." I held and squeezed his hand.

"I was told that we only kill those who commit heinous crimes. And until recently, I believed them." Archer stared at the pond, the tall grass around it swaying with the wind.

"What changed?" I asked.

"My dad didn't die in the war. My mom didn't abandon me." Archer shut his eyes, taking deep breaths. "The Firm killed my parents because they wanted out. Because this wasn't the life they wanted for me."

"Fuck," I whispered in disbelief. "Your parents were assassins too?"

Another nod. "And The Firm framed me so they could groom me."

His revelations were like tiny bombs. "Are they aware that you know?"

"Does it fucking matter?" Archer balled his fists, punching the ground. He was coiled so tightly that I feared the slightest movement could cause him to snap.

"What about this El Jefe guy? Did he have anything to do with your parents' and friends' deaths?"

"No," he answered. "And that was just the beginning, Heath."

"What do you mean?"

"They're killing innocent people. I was sent on an assignment last year. We usually don't ask details about the targets, aside from the basics, you know, but I started to question everything after finding out shit about me and my parents." His piercing eyes were back on me. "The target's descriptions, the when and the where are all the details we're given."

"Was there something special about this hit?"

"He wasn't like the previous targets. My instincts told me

things didn't add up. Remember that congressman from New Mexico last year? The one who had his opponent killed right before the election?"

"A little. I remember it was near my parish and all over the news. But I was dealing with some family issues at the time and don't remember all the details."

"Well, someone leaked emails and text messages to the press, proving the congressman was involved in his opponent's murder, but he never went to trial—"

"Because he was found dead in his cell." I completed his statement. "I remember that. They claimed it was suicide." The news outlet broke the news and it gathered national attention. According to the reports, the congressman had hung himself using a bedsheet.

"I believe he was killed because a trial would expose The Firm's ties to Congress."

"Do you have proof of that?"

"Yeah. See, that's where it gets complicated. The Firm tracked the person responsible for outing the dead congressman and that man was my assignment. He was part of The Firm. He was one of us."

"Why would The Firm do that to their own?"

"Because he knew too much and he betrayed The Firm."

"Did you believe him?"

He nodded. "He was my friend, and he showed me a transcript of the communication between the congressman and The Firm. The Firm sent me to kill him because he knew too much."

"Did you kill him?"

Archer's eyes darkened. "We need to go," he said. He stood and headed back to the small cottage. He yanked open the door, marching inside.

"Archer, wait!" I called, following him. "I thought we were staying the night?"

"It's best if we don't." He picked up his shirt from the floor, then hastily yanked it over his head. Next he tucked his gun into his waistband. "Get ready," he ordered. "I'll wait outside."

"One last question," I said.

Archer stopped by the door, glancing in my direction.

"How certain are you about The Firm?"

"Certain enough to stake my life on it. They sent people to silence me the only way they know how. I will expose them if it's the last thing I do."

He made his way outside, leaving me with my own thoughts running hundreds of miles per hour.

Twenty-Six: The Reaper

"Fuck! Fuck! Fuck!" I punched the seat of my bike. God, I was so stupid. I couldn't believe I spilled my guts to Heath like that. What I did was careless and dangerous. At least I had the smarts to get the hell out of there before I said any more. What was it about him that gave me a sense of security? Heath was the last person I could go to in case my life was in danger. He was a priest, for fuck's sake. What would he do, pray away the assassins who were after me? I needed to do damage control, and there's only one way this could end.

I have to kill him.

The ride back to Boston was quiet, tension disguised as silence. The air was filled with unspoken questions, but neither one of us uttered a word. The city approached and dread took residence in my gut, knowing that, after tonight, whatever pull Heath had on me would have to end—one way or the other. His home came into view and I stopped at the curb out front.

He didn't move.

I opened my mouth to speak, but stopped before the first word came out.

Heath tapped my stomach. "Thank you," he whispered in

my ear. The warmth of his breath tickled my skin. He hopped off the bike, released his secured bag, and then walked away without looking back.

My eyes bounced between my new apartment and the priest. *Fuck it.* Not wanting this evening to end, I followed. He was in deep thought when I sneaked in behind him. I opted to walk behind the tall shrubs to hide from the security camera I knew was pointed in my direction. My legs bumped the empty trash bin, causing it to fall on its side. "Damn it!"

Heath jogged over to check out the disturbance.

"The extremes you orchestrate to get my attention are alarming," he said when he realized it was me.

I closed the short distance between us. My eyes fixated on his lips and then traveled to the veins running parallel down his neck. I wanted a last taste of this forbidden fruit.

"You could've just said 'I'm back,'" he added, stifling a laugh.

"Yeah," I said. "But where's the fun in that?"

"Wanna come in?" he asked. "Or do you prefer breaking in? I can pretend."

I raised an eyebrow. "After you," I said, motioning to the house.

His lips were on mine the second he closed the door. We kissed like we were submerged in water and our tongues were oxygen.

Heath pulled back. "Does breaking in here and stalking me get you off?" he asked. "Of course, I know you've been here." He yanked my neck, my lips colliding with his mouth, tasting blood.

I ripped his shirt off, buttons flying, revealing his impeccable chest. I lowered my face and nipped at one nipple while my hand pinched the other. I slid off his shirt and jacket, *my jacket*,

TWENTY-SIX: THE REAPER

and continued my tease.

He moaned.

"You love that, don't you?" I looked up and met his glassy eyes. His hands caressed my jaw before he pulled me in for a deep kiss. I ground my hips against his. I pulled back from the kiss, undoing his belt.

He slid his shoes off and let his pants drop to the floor. "You're so sexy," he said, running his hand along the length of my cock before unbuttoning my jeans.

I held his hand before he was able to undress me fully. "Bed. Now," I ordered. "Ass up."

"You are a tease, Archer," he said, rushing to his bedroom.

I followed, and as instructed, he was on all fours on the bed, ass up, ready for my cock.

I grabbed the hem of my shirt and pulled it over my head before stepping out of my pants. I retrieved a condom and lube from my pocket, ripped the foil wrapper and slid the condom on, dripping lube on my shaft. I gave my cock one more stroke before lining it up with his hole.

He opened wide and let me feed him. I stared down at his opening and marveled as I watched the full length effortlessly slide inside him.

"Oh, that feels amazing," he moaned, his voice muffled by the comforter.

"It feels fucking amazing to be inside you, Heath. Fucking insane."

He grunted in response as our bodies pumped and writhed. We were two hungry guys chasing our release. Heath let out a guttural moan, toes curling as I felt my load getting ready to explode. He grabbed my ass and pulled me hard. I was balls deep in his ass when I spilled my cum into the condom.

It'd come out of nowhere. So hard and fast that I saw spots. I reached for Heath's dick and started jacking him off as I continued to nail him.

He stiffened. "Oh god!" he screamed, his cock twitching in my grip right before he flooded the sheet with his seed. We were both breathing heavily and fell onto our backs, side by side. Heath moved closer, resting his head on my chest. His hands caressed my face, my arms, my pecs. The tenderness was foreign, but I succumbed to his touch. I let him place me under his spell, and the momentary bliss was replaced by an overwhelming longing I had suppressed and ignored.

I felt like I had a giant ulcer in my stomach, or I was having a heart attack. Whatever it was, I was fucking sick.

"Where did you go? You've been quiet." Heath must've sensed my uneasiness. He looked at my face, his brows furrowing. "What's wrong?"

"Move," I said, pushing him away and running to the bathroom. I locked the door behind me. The urge to vomit had me bracing my hands on the cool porcelain sink. Dry heaving, nothing came out of my mouth but air and spit. My heart raced and I could barely breathe.

Heath knocked on the door. "Archer, are you okay?" The shadows of his feet darkened the sliver of space between the floor and the door. "Open up."

"Go away," I coughed. The absurdity of my demand didn't register until I realized that I was the intruder. I splashed cold water on my face but it didn't cool the burning spots where he'd touched me, kissed me.

"Archer, please!" His knocking became louder.

I turned, yanking the door open. I needed to get the fuck out of here.

TWENTY-SIX: THE REAPER

"What happened?" Heath asked.

I paced his bedroom, my hands pulling my hair. Somewhere during our fuck fest it had started raining, and the pounding of my heart matched the tempo of the drops tapping the window. I was going crazy. I needed my old life back.

"Archer." He stood in front of me and placed his hands on my shoulders. "What happened?"

I swatted his hands away and moved as far as I could from him until my back was against the wall. "You fucking happened."

He tried to grab me, but I raised my hand, stopping him.

"Don't," I barked. I picked up my scattered clothes, then hurriedly put them on. "I have to go."

"What's going on?" Heath wrapped himself in his robe, yanking my shirt from my hand to get my attention.

"Give me that," I ordered, stepping toward him. I was surprised when he stood his ground. "I said …" Our faces were inches apart, his blue eyes begging for answers. Answers I didn't have. "Give me that," I repeated. My lips brushed the tip of his nose.

"Or what?" He puffed his chest as if preparing to fight.

"You don't want to find out. Give it." Our chests were heaving in unison.

"Make me." His determination was hard as steel.

I reached for the shirt but Heath tucked it behind him. My hands wrapped around his neck, lifting his chin. "Don't say I didn't warn you."

He tossed the shirt to the floor in front of the unmade king-size bed. Heath pulled me closer to his face.

I pushed him away; his body slammed into the lamp behind him, the brass base making a hollow clunk when it hit the floor, causing the light to go out. I walked toward the shirt, but Heath jumped on my back, causing both of us to fall with a smack. He was on top of me and had me in a headlock, and was able to pin one of my arms behind my back. The fucker's strength was still surprising. I wiggled, but his grip tightened. If I didn't know any better, I would've thought he was trying to suffocate me. I bucked my hips, extending my hand to stand without any success.

Finally, I elbowed his side. He grunted, and his grip loosened. It was the window I needed to flip the script. I grabbed his right hand, twisting it around his back. I pinned his head with my knee.

He bent his knee, slamming his heel into my nuts.

"Fuck!" I screamed, landing on my side, cupping my balls.

He stood and staggered away.

"You're gonna fucking pay for that," I spat. I grabbed his leg, tripping him. His body rammed the edge of the bed. Heath kicked my face and, seconds later, I tasted metal. He was determined to stop me, I'd give him that, but I was just warming up.

I pulled his hair, exposing his neck. There was a cut on his left brow, and a bruise on his cheek. "Having fun?" I asked.

"You have no idea." Heath butted my head with his and escaped my grasp.

It hurt like a son of a bitch, and I touched my head to see if I was bleeding too.

When I finally focused on him, his fist was loaded and ready to swing.

"Where did you learn how to fight?" I asked, taking the first swing, missing.

"There are a lot of things you don't know about me," he said.

TWENTY-SIX: THE REAPER

We walked in circles, flinching whenever one of us threw a punch. A combo hook and a jab connected with his face. That combo would knock out most men, but not him. Heath saw an opening and kicked my side, followed by a punch to my jaw that caused me to stagger to my knees.

The fucker knew what he was doing.

I leapt from the ground and tackled his waist. Gravity pulled us to the floor. "I can do this forever," I said, sitting on top of him. He reached for the fallen lamp and bashed my head with it. My vision was invaded by black spots. I glanced behind the nightstand, searching for my gun, where I'd placed it earlier.

Heath's eyes bounced between me and the gun. No one moved as we each calculated our next attack.

The rain had eased, and there was now a rustling outside that caught my attention, followed by a loud slamming of a door.

Heath beelined to his dresser and yanked it open. I ran to pick up my gun, turning and aiming it at the door, when I suddenly stopped cold. "What the fuck?" I said. Heath was holding a pistol, aimed at my head. "You gonna fucking shoot me?" I redirected my gun to him.

He shrugged.

"Who the fuck are you?"

Something hard and cold hit the back of my head. I fell to the ground. Heath's face melted into black.

Twenty-Seven: The Priest

The Reaper was my mission.

The Church operated under the claws of The Firm. Decades ago, their merger solidified The Firm's power and strengthened their stranglehold on the underground world. We were The Priests, a group of trained assassins passed on down our family's generations. Our modus operandi was simple and yet extraordinarily effective. We committed ourselves to a lifelong servitude to the Catholic Church, and in return we were rewarded with a sum of money we wouldn't be able to spend in our lifetime. We went to the seminary like any other priest, but our similarities ended there. Our lethal skills were cloaked by our robes, disguised by our service. I learned to like what I did, but at the end of the day, it was a facade, a charade that would have to end one way or the other.

I was sent to Boston to kill someone. I didn't know that someone was Archer. The Reaper. Until today.

I stared at Archer's unconscious body and wondered why the Church had waited this long to reveal the identity of my assignment. Would that have mattered? Perhaps. It would've been easier to have known from the beginning, before Archer revealed his identity to me and what he knew about The Firm. And I believed him, which added a layer of complication to this mission. *What am I going to do now?*

After Archer made the decision to head back to Boston, I sent a text to Archbishop Llyod to notify him I would secure the target tonight. When he responded that he would send reinforcements, an unsettling doubt consumed me as we neared the city. It was too late to back away. Not that the Church or The Firm would let me anyway.

My assignment in Albuquerque ended tragically, and the reason for the church to send backup was justified. I didn't have a flawless track record, unlike The Reaper. According to his file, he was an expert at pretty much everything required to succeed at our job. Hand-to-hand combat? Check. Long-range shooting? Check. Intel gathering and lip reading? Check and check.

The case he mentioned about the congressman from New Mexico was assigned to me. It was an easy task. A corrupt politician getting rid of his opponent? I could do that without breaking a sweat. The congressman was a parish donor so access to him wouldn't be an issue, and I became complacent. Andrew's disappearance had momentarily taken my eyes off the assignment, and before I knew it, a whistleblower had outed the congressman and he was taken into custody. I scrambled to find a way to take him out from his prison cell, but The Firm was impatient, so they took the matter into their own hands. The next thing I knew, I was being relocated to Boston with a failed mission and a missing brother.

I didn't know The Firm's involvement with the death of the congressman's opponent until Archer told me. Just how corrupt was The Firm? Were they the reason for Andrew's disappearance? I shook the thought out of my head; I refused to accept the idea that he was gone. Archer was the last person standing between me and a successful mission. I'd focus on finding Andrew when this was over.

"Great job, Father Saint James," one of the three backup men said. They were not priests. We were not the same. "Where do you wanna finish this?" he asked, pointing at Archer.

The Reaper, who'd spent half of his life serving The Firm, was reduced to *this*. Conflicted, I focused my attention on Archer. I wanted to buy more time before I made the kill. "We can't do it here," I said. "It's too risky."

"Okay, so where?"

"Take him here." I showed the men the address to one of the Church's properties outside the city where most killings took place. I pulled the nightstand open, grabbed a set of keys, and tossed them over.

The three swapped glances before nodding. "We can do that," the other man said. "Here, cuff him." He threw handcuffs to his buddy, who kneeled and restrained Archer's hands. "This fucker is The Reaper. He can kill us with his bare hands."

I winced at the way he tugged on Archer's arms. "I'll follow you," I said as they exited the bedroom. Until I remembered something. "Wait," I called.

The men dragging Archer from their shoulders stopped.

I stood in front of them, glancing at Archer's face. "I need this." I fished his motorcycle key and cell phone from his pocket, fighting the urge to touch his wobbling head. Once they were gone, I rushed to the office, pulling a briefcase from under the bookshelf. After entering the combination in the lock, it popped open, revealing my favorite selection of firearms. I tucked two of them in my waistband and wrapped

TWENTY-SEVEN: THE PRIEST

one with a holder around my ankle. I headed to my computer and plugged in the USB, reopening the file. I dialed Andrew's number in hopes of reaching him. I needed his guidance more than ever. "Please pick up," I murmured. It went to voice mail.

It was as if my head was about to split from aching after minutes of figuring out what the hundreds of names and numbers were for, their significance, and what to do with Archer. I slammed my hand on the desk. I didn't have time to dwell on this. I ejected and pocketed the file before rushing out, halting to pick up Archer's leather jacket from the floor.

A dull ache stabbed my heart at seeing Archer's bike on the street. His scent intoxicated my senses when I put his helmet on. The moments we'd shared flashed in my head, his revelations echoed in my soul. *I have to do what I have to do.* I pressed the ignition. The sound of the motor cut through the quiet street. Torn between my mission and Archer, I sped up.

The starless tar-colored sky opened again, the rain it had been holding fell just as I reached the location. I ran for cover, heading to the house. A black Suburban SUV was parked in the driveway of the Cape Cod-style bungalow. It was dark inside, and the only lights visible from the street were coming from the open basement window. The wind blew heavy raindrops sideways through it.

Passing by the parked vehicle, I peeked inside and found tactical and rifle bags on the back seat. *That's a little overkill*, I told myself. But then again, we were dealing with The Reaper. On the floor of the SUV were black body bags.

My phone vibrated, and I glanced at the screen as I stepped under an awning: Andrew. I hurried to answer the call but, like the last time, all I could hear was static and beeping. "Andrew?" I whispered. I couldn't be sure one of the men wasn't around, listening.

Footsteps and chatter coming from inside the house drew my attention, forcing me disconnect the call.

"I can't believe we got him," one of the men said.

"The Reaper my ass," the other chided.

I shook my head. The only reason they were able to get him was because they caught him off guard. The sight of me holding a gun had disarmed him, gauging by the look of surprise on Archer's face before he dropped unconscious. The ache in my chest returned, gripping my heart tighter.

Their voices faded. Another car pulled in behind the SUV and two armed men exited the vehicle.

"Wait up here," I ordered. "I'll call if we need backup."

It was time to finish what I'd started.

Twenty-Eight: The Reaper

I was awakened by the sound of dripping water hitting glass. Its rhythm was slow but steady. My chin was pressed against what felt like cold concrete. My clothes were wet and clinging to my body, and I shivered to stay warm. I tried to open my eyes, but my eyelids stayed shut. My hands were immovable against metal behind my back. *Handcuffs.* I attempted to shift my body, but only managed to lift my head. A rush of pain hit the back of my head like a motherfucker, and I groaned. *Fuck.*

I listened intently to my surroundings, trying to get my bearings. It was raining, and there were people in the room. The haze in my thoughts began to clear and memories came rushing back all at once.

We made love.

We fought.

There was a loud noise.

Heath pointed a gun at me.

No. He wouldn't. He couldn't. He must have been pointing it at the intruders. Were they after me? Or him?

My heart hammered in my chest at the thought. Where the fuck was Heath? These fuckers had better not've hurt him, or

I would make their lives a living hell.

I forced my eyes open; pain cut through as if they were being ripped in two. Blurry boots and legs appeared when I managed to open my eyes a sliver. Their conversation was too faint to make out. I wished I could see their lips.

A taste of salt and iron hit the back of my mouth when I swallowed. My vision started to sharpen and I realized that the floor was covered with blood and rainwater.

Before I could wonder whose blood I was lying in, a muddy boot pressed against my shoulder and shoved so hard I was forced onto my back.

"He's awake," the genius with muddy boots announced.

Three ugly faces I didn't recognize were staring at me with smug smiles.

"Look who's finally up," said the one sporting a beer belly. His grating high-pitched voice didn't match his stocky appearance.

I wriggled in an attempt to free myself, but the handcuffs between my back and the concrete cut into my skin. "Fuck you!" I croaked, spitting blood at their feet.

One of the men dashed toward me, driving a kick to my stomach. "I wouldn't be cocky if I were you," he said.

I gasped from the pain, and coughed up blood and spit. "You better hope I don't get out of here—"

"Or what?" the short guy interrupted with a kick to my head. "The Reaper is gonna hunt me down?"

The Reaper? What the fuck? How did these clowns know who I was? "The Firm sent you fuckers?" I asked, hoping for some answers. "I should be offended."

"And why is that?" the stocky dude asked.

"Sending the bottom of the barrel to get me? That fucking

hurts more than your pussy blows."

"What did you say, motherfucker? I should kill you right now." He balled his fists and marched toward me, but his buddy grabbed his hand.

"Where is Father Saint James?" I asked.

"He's not here, lover boy," Stocky said, looking disgusted. He spit on my face and snarled. "Fucking fags."

"Shut up, dude," Shorty warned Stocky. "Just shut up."

The spit dripping down my cheek was as rank as I suspected. I just needed an opening to escape and find Heath. "What are you gonna do now?" I asked, taunting the stocky guy with a short fuse. Perhaps egging him on would make him talk. "Or are you waiting for big daddy to tell you good little boys how to handle the big bad assassins?"

"Shut the fuck up!" he yelled. His face was red, fuming. "Stand up!"

The muddy boot released me, but I didn't move. I maintained awareness of my location, trying to figure out a way to get the hell out of this situation. These men didn't have the authority to kill me, otherwise I would've been dead already.

"Help him." Shorty elbowed the other guy, who looked average as fuck with his pale face and thinning brown hair.

He gave him a questioning look, a little terrified of the prospect of being near me. Was it The Firm who'd sent those men who ambushed me in Havana? That couldn't be. El Jefe swore he didn't know.

I grimaced when two of the guys each grabbed an elbow.

Thanks to their help, I was able to take stock of my surroundings. We were definitely in an unfinished basement. The room was bare, a wooden frame outlined the walls, exposing electrical wires and copper pipes. To my right was a dilapidated eight-step stairway leading up. The spaces where windows should be were boarded up, except for the open one.

The two men's eyes were on me as they lifted my body from the concrete floor. A mixture of curiosity and fear reflected in their shaky gazes.

"Boo!" I tried to make a move forward, not to escape because I wasn't stupid enough to pull an act like that without a plan, but to rattle them. It worked; they staggered back, almost falling in the process.

"Bunch of fucking babies," I said, chuckling.

Stocky swung a fist, making contact with my cheek.

It hurt like a son of a bitch, but I was in a psychological war, so I smiled at him. "Is that the best you got?" Why had they sent these guys to kill me instead of the dozens of lethal assassins they had in their arsenal? To be honest, I was insulted. Was this a test? Or were they afraid I'd start killing the cream of the crop? These three were too jumpy to be considered real threats. "Before I kill you, tell me where Heath is."

"You just wait and see." Another glare from Stocky promised empty threats.

"Enough!" Shorty said, walking closer to face me. "I should kill you now and be done with it," he said through gritted teeth.

"You can try. I'm not afraid of death, and definitely not afraid of you three sorry nut sacks," I taunted. I needed him to get messy so I could finish this and escape. I could already see the fear in their eyes. "Just make sure you actually kill me, because I'm going to enjoy having fun with all of you."

Seeing the other two look at each other with wide eyes was the cherry on top. I couldn't hide the laughter that bubbled up from the insanity I'd nurtured for the past decade. To

TWENTY-EIGHT: THE REAPER

really drive home my point, I spit in Shorty's face. The mix of phlegm, blood, and saliva dripping over his eye was an extremely satisfying sight.

He was about to throw a hook when the door upstairs slammed open. The dilapidated steps creaked from the weight of the slowly descending newcomer.

Based on the change among the three goons, this was someone important. Shorty backed away, his hands balled at his sides. I thought they were afraid of me, but whoever was descending those steps inspired respect and invoked fear from these men.

I twisted painfully between the two holding me up, preparing myself to fight. They were distracted and this was the opening I needed.

But when I saw the handsome man at the bottom of the stairs wearing my leather jacket, my plans crashed and burned.

"Heath?" I asked. An icy chill washed over me as I put two and two together. I knew there was something different about him, but my obsession with him clouded my judgment.

I'd been played.

Fuck!

And I had spilled my guts to him. I trusted him. I'd told him things I'd never told anyone. I hoped to fucking god he'd leave my grandparents alone. The thought of something happening to them made my blood boil. I was so fucking blind.

"What happened to his face?" he asked one of the men.

"What do you fucking care? It's not like we're gonna be fucking anymore," I barked. I couldn't believe I'd been betrayed again. First Wolf, now Heath? My chest hurt so bad it felt like my heart was beating around an icepick.

"Release him," Heath ordered, commanding the men to

uncuff my hands. His eyes never left mine, but I couldn't read behind the veil of impassivity. Were any of the things he'd told me true? Or were they all part of his plan? He was so stoic and calm, I felt a twinge of panic.

The Priests. I'd heard about them, of course, because they were more elusive than me. They were lineage assassins that could be traced back to the Crusades. An invisible spearhead of the Catholic Church. They were ruthless.

I was in trouble.

"No wonder you're so good at fucking," I taunted, to hide the rage and fear brewing inside.

Heath took a deep breath. "Release him," he repeated.

"Are you sure?" Stocky asked, a frown on his face.

"Yes," Heath said, still staring at me. His features softened to the one I'd come to know. "We'll let him die with dignity."

Hesitantly, Stocky fished the keys out of his pockets. They dangled at his side, rattling when he neared me. His hands were trembling, perhaps from the prospect of cutting me loose.

I smirked at Stocky, waggling my eyebrows before I returned my attention back to the real monster in the room. "Why'd they send you to kill me?" I asked. I wanted to hear it from him. I'd been careful, making sure that only a handful of people knew of my plan to expose The Firm.

"You know why," Heath whispered.

"Yeah, fucker," Shorty piped in, interrupting adult conversation.

I doubted the three unfortunate souls understood who they shared a basement with.

Heath snarled at him, and that seemed to be the only sign Shorty needed to shut the hell up. "We can't let you destroy

TWENTY-EIGHT: THE REAPER

what we've built, Reaper," he explained.

My hands were released; rings of raw pink skin were etched into my wrists.

The men—except Heath—retreated and drew their guns, aiming them in my direction, adding wrinkles to my very limited plan. I could tackle those guys, but Heath was the wildcard that made me hesitate. After our little tussle earlier that evening, he was more dangerous than all three goons and their guns combined.

"You see…" Heath closed the distance between us. His hands were in his pockets. "The success of The Firm depends on our ability to stay under the radar, and we can't have men like you going rogue on us." He shook his head. "We can't risk it."

"Do you believe me?" I asked. I had to know. I thought I could trust him, but what did I know? "Do you believe me?" I balled my fists, ready to die fighting. I finally had a purpose and I would fight until the end.

Heath didn't answer. The three men behind him exchanged confused looks, clearly wondering what I was talking about.

"Let's just get this over with," Shorty urged.

"So, do you?" I yelled, my frustration growing. If these fuckers thought I'd lay down and take what they were going to give, they couldn't have been more wrong.

Heath stayed silent and reached out a hand in the men's direction. After a short pause, Stocky handed over his pistol.

He stepped forward, his eyes never leaving mine. He unzipped his jacket—*my* leather jacket—to reveal two guns tucked into the sides of his waistband. He took another step, stopping within arm's reach of me. He raised his arm and pointed his gun at my chest. *Read my lips,* he mouthed.

What the fuck? I glared at him, my eyes focused on the lips I had enjoyed kissing a few hours ago.

Blink if you can read my lips.

I squinted briefly, hoping to relay the message.

"What are you waiting for?" Stocky yelled. His high voice was strained with impatience, and I saw him step forward in my periphery.

"I got this!" Heath replied. His lips started to move, soundless words coming out. *There are two more guys outside.*

My gaze traveled to the stairs, then back to his. *Your bike is parked across the street.*

My heart was pounding so hard, but my mind was clear. I knew what I had to do. Heath was risking this for me.

On three.

I blinked.

One. He glanced at the guns tucked into his waistband.

Two.

I nodded.

Three.

I pulled both guns out just as he was turning.

He shot one of the men directly in the forehead. A thud when his body hit the ground.

"What the fu—" The second bullet hit Shorty before he had a chance to finish his statement.

I took down Stocky with one bullet to his temple and made my way to the stairs.

The door slammed open, light from upstairs illuminating me at the bottom of the steps. Two guys rushed down and Heath and I took them one at a time.

I aimed my gun at Heath. He aimed his at me. Neither of us flinched a muscle.

"Run," Heath said. "There are more coming." He pulled my

keys and burner phone out of his pocket, tossing them to me.

"You're not coming with me?"

"No, I have to answer for this," he whispered.

What would happen to him when I escaped? My feet were planted next to the dead guy with a lit cigarette still dangling from his lips, debating what to do. I hated that I cared about what they would do to Heath, but the thought of having someone torture or kill him wasn't sitting well with me.

"Archer, go, or I'll have to kill you," he threatened, aiming Shorty's gun at my face for the second time tonight.

It was a bluff and we both knew it.

He fired his gun inches to the left, hitting the wall behind me. "Go, please."

"So, you believe me?"

"I do."

"Then come with me."

Heath shook his head. "I can't, Archer."

"Why?" He had to—they wouldn't have mercy on him.

"To deal with the consequences and to buy you more time." He motioned his gun around the dead bodies on the floor. "Just go!"

Two steps brought us face-to-face. I grabbed a fistful of his hair and pulled his face to mine, kissing him. "Damn you, Heath!"

I ran.

Twenty-Nine: The Priest

Three assignments and three failures. My negligence and incompetence to secure a target proved, once and for all, that I wasn't cut out for this life. The life I never wanted for myself. I tolerated it because of my brother, my only family, and I wasn't even sure I still had him. Andrew and I knew the consequences of betraying the Church and The Firm, we'd seen it firsthand. I thought I was an assassin, but I wasn't. Not even close.

I'd like to believe that believing Archer and the things he'd exposed about The Firm was the only reason I let him go, but the truth lay deeper than I'd ever wanted to admit. There was something about him that fascinated me. He was a living contradiction. He was lethal, no doubt about it, but it was his principles and the way he was willing to die for what he believed in that made me admire him even more.

I stared at the five lifeless bodies swimming in pools of blood and rainwater on the concrete floor and shook my head. If it wasn't for the dire situation in front of me, I would've laughed at the irony of it all. This failure was my ultimate success. A mission within a mission. If Archer could expose The Firm, then all this would have been worth it—including my own life.

TWENTY-NINE: THE PRIEST

I told Archer once that I wasn't afraid to die, because I wasn't. What I was afraid of was leaving this world without making a mark, big or small. I wanted to matter.

I sat on the basement floor with my back against the cold wall, listening to the rain's melody while I waited for the rest of The Firm's minions. They would be here to collect The Reaper's body. Archer should be far away by then. He was fighting against an institution, but if there was anyone who could find the chinks in The Firm's armor, I hoped it was him.

Headlights glowed from outside, the beams sweeping across the open window accompanied by the crunching of tires over the gravel driveway. Loud footsteps shuddered the ceiling above as they marched to the basement. Legs appeared on the exposed steps. I stopped counting after four pairs. Their faces emerged, eyes wide, jaws dropped in disbelief. Some of the men were wearing black robes, while the others donned maroon cassocks.

"What happened here?" one of them asked. I recognized him immediately: it was the same man who'd escorted me when I met Archbishop Lloyd. He scanned the room before his gaze landed on me. "The Church will be disappointed in your failure," he said quietly, his eyes taking in the dead goons before falling on me again. "You'll have to answer for your sins."

"I know."

He motioned toward me and two men came forward.

I was sure I could take them, but I was tired of killing.

The man in charge pulled out a cell phone from his cassock and pressed the screen before holding the phone to his ear. "The Bishop has failed. The Reaper lives." He listened and nodded; a minute passed. "Your orders regarding The Bishop?"

Pause. "Okay."

Two of the men pulled me to my feet, gripping both of my arms. "Did you do all this?" the man on my right asked, tying my hands with zip ties.

I didn't respond. It wouldn't make a difference. The conclusion of this mission had been determined.

"He's coming with us," the man on the phone said before hanging up. He looked around the basement one last time before shaking his head in disappointment. "This is a mess. Call for extra body bags and make sure this is all cleaned up before sunrise."

Someone pushed me from behind, causing me to fall to one knee. "Hurry the fuck up," he said and pulled my hair, while the other man yanked my shirt, forcing me to stand.

I followed the men outside. My heart dropped. Archer's motorcycle remained parked where I'd left it. I scanned the perimeter. A shadow appeared behind one of the trees lining the street, almost invisible, but I knew that outline. It was Archer wearing his helmet, watching us.

No one else noticed him. Maybe because they overestimated his desire to live. I hoped he wouldn't do anything stupid. But The Reaper didn't get his name by playing it safe. Realizing that I was staring, I turned my attention to the gravel driveway, and prayed that he wouldn't get involved right now.

Another black SUV stopped in front of the house. Three men in white hazmat suits exited the vehicle, nodding in our direction as they passed. I risked a glance back at Archer.

I shook my head slightly, hoping he would pick up on my signal, until someone placed a black cloth bag over my head and shoved me inside the van. My head hit something hard and plastic, and I groaned. Another person yanked on my shirt to keep me upright. Something warm dripped from my forehead to my cheek and then down to my lips. I stuck my tongue out and tasted blood. We drove off, and I prayed to God Archer didn't follow us. There was a bigger pursuit than saving me. I was beyond saving.

After what seemed like forever on the road, the SUV slowed to a stop. The sound of a window rolling down was followed by buzzing. "It's us," someone said.

A second later, a metal gate rattled as it swung open, and we drove on.

The men pulled me out of the van with zero finesse. "We got it from here," someone said, jabbing me with what I could only assume was the barrel of a gun.

"I can't believe this guy is The Cardinal's brother," another voice said. Andrew was The Cardinal, one of the best of our kind. "Move," he urged with another jab. I was nothing like my brother. Andrew was a great assassin. One of the best Priests the Church had ever produced.

Being pushed and tugged, I blindly tripped down hundreds of steps. Even with the bag over my head, I could feel the chill in the air. The men's voices bounced around, our footsteps and heavy breathing echoed. Stale air laced with the decay that always accompanied death penetrated the cloth.

The bag was pulled over my head and my eyes took a minute to adjust. We were standing in a dark narrow hallway, with cells on both sides. I knew this kind of place. We were deep underground, in an old cave that had been retrofitted to lock away those awaiting torture. I figured no one would hear my screams, if I lived long enough to be tortured. The walls are roughly carved from stone and were covered with mold and dried bodily fluids I didn't want to think about. Across from the cells was an open space with a single torch lodged in the wall that illuminated thick manacles hanging from the ceiling and old rusted tools arranged on a table. This was a barbaric place where crimes against humanity thrived.

A man I didn't recognize cut the zip ties, freeing my hands. The tight plastic left deep impressions in my skin. He pulled the keys hanging from his belt and opened the cell. The men dragged me inside then bound both of my wrists with rusty chains.

"Where am I?" I asked.

"Hell," he uttered before walking away, locking me inside.

***

A slap woke me. I blinked my eyes, trying to focus on the people inside my cell. It was a lot brighter now; someone was holding a torch over me. A man pulled an old crank, and the chain attached to the thick rusted manacles clamped around my wrists tightened and screeched. The metal against metal noise made me wince. As the crank moved, my arms were pulled into the air, the rest of my body lifting off the ground. While I dangled helplessly, my legs were placed in similar restraints.

I looked at each face, hoping to see someone I recognized. Maybe some empathy. Archbishop Lloyd materialized from the shadows. His slit eyes and scrunched nose showed his distaste. Distaste in me. He clasped his hands just above his stomach as he walked around my suspended body, the gold chain around his neck with the palm-sized crucifix catching the torch light.

When he was in front of me again, I stared at the gold Jesus.

TWENTY-NINE: THE PRIEST

"Forgive me, Father, for I have si—"

He slapped my face with the back of his hand. "You are pathetic," he said. "But I can't say I'm surprised."

"You lied to me," I barked.

The archbishop slapped me again, one of his sharp rings cutting my cheek this time. "Who asked you to speak? Look at you," he said, spitting to his side. "I'd hoped that a relative of The Cardinal would be a force to be reckoned with. Yet not once, but three times, you've failed a mission." He pulled a white handkerchief from an inner pocket of his white robe then used it to wipe my blood off his gaudy ring. "What a waste. The Reaper. He is one of The Firm's best assets with his natural talent for killing. But you should have been better." A humorless laugh escaped his mouth. "But he stuck his nose in something that didn't belong." He stopped pacing and brought his attention to me. "And I'm not talking about you." Another slap. "I didn't know you're a faggot until I saw those pictures of you and him. I should've suspected it based on your pathetic performance. Your family would be ashamed of you."

"Leave them out of this. This is between you and me."

Archbishop Lloyd ignored me and continued with his tirade. "Real men tackle the mission head-on. Your brother was great at that. He was a Priest through and through. He'd go on an assignment and deal with his target without hesitation." He walked to the corner of the cell block and grabbed something hanging on the wall. "Take his shirt off," he ordered.

Within seconds, someone scurried toward me and ripped my shirt in half, letting the fabric hang off my arms.

When he turned toward me, I saw the flogger bouncing in his hand as he tested its weight. This was going to hurt.

"Being a Priest is a privilege." The archbishop closed the

gap between us, the black leather flogger with a serrated end contrasting with his clean white robes. "We are committed to cleansing humanity of their sins." He walked behind me. "Why else do we go through the hoops of sending you through seminary to become an ordained assassin?"

Then he lashed my back.

I howled, my voice echoing against the stone walls.

"Because the success of our missions lies in our ability to blend in. Unlike your little boyfriend. Archer, is it?" Another snap of his wrist, and leather ripped across my back.

The pain was excruciating. Sweat trickled down my face and saliva dripped down my chin.

"Anyone can do what The Reaper does. But us …" He walked around and faced me. "We are ordained by God the Almighty." He lashed my chest twice; splatters of blood landed on my face after the second time.

"No one can do what The Reaper can," I barked. That was the truth: he was one of a kind.

"Certainly not you." He flogged my stomach and my sides, over and over.

I closed my eyes, lightheaded from the pain. I wanted to cry out, but I refused to give him the satisfaction of breaking me. Men like him loved inflicting pain and got off on their victims' agony. I gritted my teeth and glared at him. "I never wanted to be part of this. Any of this."

His hand stopped midair. Rage filled his gaze. "Remember when I told you choice is an illusion? Your parents didn't have a choice. You and your brother were promised to the Church the moment you were born," he explained, reminding me of our first conversation. "They could've stopped with Andrew really. We just wanted one to replace your father. But no, he got greedy."

I'd never heard this before. "What do you mean?"

"They had to have another to pay off his debts. He had this illusion of *retiring*, so they had another kid—and that's you."

"So you had them killed because they wanted out?"

"They retired." A sinister grin graced his face. "Andrew was always worried about you. Someone had to, since your folks never did."

"You're lying," I said.

"Archbishops never lie." He chuckled. "Now, back to your failure. We know how deadly The Reaper is so … we sent you."

The mention of Archer caused my heart to drop and my stomach to unsettle. "You sent me to him … to die?"

"You were supposed to be just a distraction while the real Priests took him down. So imagine my surprise when you got him and almost succeeded." He handed the flogger to one of his men. Relief washed over me. "But just like the last two times, you failed again. This one though …" He waved his finger at me. "This one takes the cake."

"Just kill me and get this over with."

A monk entered wearing a brown robe with a hood. His head was bowed, and in the dim room I couldn't see his face. He moved to the side, blending into the darkness.

"Who said anything about killing you? We don't kill our kind. We don't take innocent lives. You know that."

He was full of crap. I used to believe that, but not anymore. *Did I used to sound this certifiable too?*

"Well, I'll give you an opportunity to repent. Tell me where The Reaper is and I will absolve you of your sins."

Like that was going to happen. "You'll never find him. You

said it yourself, he's one of a kind." I looked directly into Archbishop Lloyd's eyes. "I'm done being your little dog. He'll find you. He'll make you all pay in ways that'll make you wish you were dead. He'll expose your connection to The Firm and destroy it all."

"Have it your way, Father Saint James. We have other ways to flush him out." He stepped closer. "I wonder how his grandparents are?" he whispered in my ear, as if it was a secret he wasn't supposed to reveal.

"Leave them out of this!" I shouted.

Archbishop Lloyd punched my stomach. "You never had what it takes to be a Priest." He walked to the corner, grabbing a shiny rod. When he turned back around, I realized what it was: a dagger in a case. He pulled it out, exposing the sharp blade. "I'm going to kill you slowly." I held my breath as he neared me, closing my eyes. I couldn't believe this was how my life was going to end.

Thirty: The Reaper

There was no fire hot enough to burn me, water deep enough to drown me. They whispered it. Sometimes, they screamed. But the sound of terror as my name was spoken on their lips when they gasped for their final breath was music to my wicked soul.

I hit the archbishop's head with the base of my gun, causing him to fall to his knees. The dagger clattered to the ground. I grabbed it and slit his throat with one swift cut to his carotid artery. He grabbed at his neck as he collapsed; blood gushed through his fingers when I leaned closer to him so my face was the last thing he saw before he went to hell. "Fuck. You," I whispered.

"The Reaper," he croaked before his head rolled to the side, his lifeless eyes wide open.

I hurried to the man behind Heath, who was trying to escape, smashing his face into a bar. He landed on his back with a loud, satisfying thud. I snatched the keys from his belt then used the crank to lower Heath to the ground.

"Who are you?" Heath asked as I unlocked the manacles. He glanced around the cell, appearing confused. He slowly pulled my hood down, grimacing at the fresh wounds marring his beautiful body. His mouth dropped. "Archer." He fell into me, wrapping his arms around my neck. We were chest to chest, heart to heart.

I held him tighter.

"What are you doing here?" he asked, shaking his head. "You should've left. What about The Firm?"

"I will deal with them later. But I couldn't bear it if anything happened to you." I studied his body when he released me from his embrace. My jaw tightened; he was covered in welts, cuts, and blood.

"It's okay." He cupped my face, urging me to meet his eyes. "Archer, I'm alive."

I nodded, but that was way too close for comfort for me. I glanced behind me, picked up the knife, and stabbed the archbishop's chest, piercing his heart for all the pain he inflicted on Heath. "He's fucking dead, and no one will ever lay their hands on you again," I promised.

I brought our faces together, our lips finding each other's. We kissed like there was no tomorrow. He quenched my thirst and fed my soul.

"How did you get in here?" he asked when our lips parted.

"I'll tell you later. We don't have much time." I undressed the unconscious man on the floor, leaving him with just his underwear on. "Wear this." I handed Heath the man's clothes.

"Is he dead?"

"No, but we have to go before he wakes up." I helped him stand and he winced, his whole body shivering. "Can you lift your arms?"

He nodded, taking deep breaths while I helped him put on the clothes.

"Take these too," I said, handing him two handguns. "My

motorcycle is parked in the woods south of here."

Heath patted his pants, searching for something. "Here it is," he said when he showed me his cell phone. "Where are we?"

"A fucking monastery in Maine," I answered. "Can you run?"

"Yeah." He tucked one of the guns in his waistband before grabbing my hand.

So we ran, tracing back the steps I'd taken to get to the dungeons.

I could finally breathe now that Heath was safe. I was so thankful I'd made it in time, that fucker was seconds from stabbing Heath with his dagger. I had so many questions for him about his involvement with The Firm, but those questions would have to wait because we had more pressing matters to worry about, like getting the fuck out of here alive. "Leave it to the Church to be so fucking barbaric," I said. "A fucking dungeon? Really? Are we in the fucking 1700s?"

"It's all about tradition, and these guys are old school," Heath answered, squirming when he pulled the shirt away from his sensitive skin.

"We're almost out of here," I said, squeezing his hand. "I'll take a look when we get out."

"I'll be okay. This is way better than the alternative." He released the magazine of his gun, checking the number of bullets while we ran.

"Zero, can you talk to me?" I said into the wireless headset in my ear. "Zero? Damn it! The reception down here is shitty," I whispered.

"Who's Zero?" he asked.

"Zero is one of The Firm's hackers. She's tracking us right now to get us out of here. She's already hacked into the security system." I called Zero while following the van here.

I'd let her in on The Firm's secrets and asked her to check for herself. And because she was the best at what she does, she was able to hack into the email address I gave her. It was from the email Heath received before we headed to New Hampshire to meet with the archbishop. I had the foresight to memorize it then.

"Okay," he said. "Where did you get your clothes?"

"The monks' quarters. That fucking place is a giant sex orgy. You should've seen what they were doing."

"I know all about that," he said.

"Based on experience?" I asked, ignoring the sudden pang of jealousy.

"Nope."

We stopped running, hiding behind the wall at the sound of pounding footsteps. "Shhh," I whispered, placing my index finger to my lips before pointing in the direction of the sound. I peeked and found a group of men running in the opposite direction. Shit was about to hit the fan, especially when they found the archbishop's body. "This way." I led the way toward the round staircase. "I'll take the top, you take the bottom," I instructed, slowly making our way up, our guns drawn.

"Reaper, do you copy?" I exhaled upon hearing Zero's voice. She was our lifeline.

"Yeah," I whispered.

"Is he with you?"

"Yes."

"Good. You're three floors below ground, so take the steps as far as you can and do it fast. There's an exit to your immediate right when you get to the top of the staircase," Zero instructed.

"How many people are guarding that exit?" I asked.

"Three men, according to the surveillance camera."

"Fuck."

"I don't like the sound of that," Heath said. "Can we make it?"

I wished I knew. "We just gotta keep going."

"Don't worry, boo, I got you," Zero said. The sounds of her keyboard carried down the line. "I'll shut down their power when you're close so you can take out the guards."

We arrived on the next floor without being noticed. "Can you do that?" I asked Zero.

"You did not just ask me that," she said.

"My bad."

"Archer, hurry! Someone's coming," Heath whispered.

Shots were fired in our direction, hitting the metal stairs. "They're over there," someone yelled. More bullets pinged against the metal around us as we ran upstairs while Heath returned fire on the men following us.

"You're almost there," Zero said.

Gunshots coming from upstairs whipped past my side, barely missing me. "Fuck!" I aimed my gun at the man looking down, shooting him in the face. He fell, landing three floors down.

"Were you hit?" Heath asked.

"No. How much longer, Zero?"

"In three, two, one. Be prepared for darkness," she said. And, on command, the lights went out. We used the rails to guide us the rest of the way up.

We slammed the exit door open and dove to the ground. Just as Zero mentioned, three men were waiting outside. They fired their guns aimlessly toward the open door, unable to see through the darkness that we were on the ground. The glow of their guns' barrels gave their location away. Heath and I took our shots. Bodies thudded, then silence. "We got them," Heath said.

We rose to our feet and ran toward the woods. "We need to protect your grandparents," Heath said between heavy breaths.

"Why?" I asked. The sprint to escape the monastery and the men who were after us made my lungs burn. "Stop for a second." I reached for his elbow, halting him. "What are you talking about?"

"The Firm is going to use them as pawns to get to you."

"Are you sure?"

Heath held my shoulders, nodding.

"God-fucking-damn it!" I kicked the ground. Fear, frustration, rage, and helplessness paralyzed my mind. My instinct was to kill, but it wouldn't do me any good at the moment. I needed to come up with a concrete plan. Fast.

"I don't know how much time we have, but it was what the Archbishop told me before you slit his throat."

My phone vibrated in my pocket. I ignored the call, focusing my attention on Heath, but it started buzzing again. I pulled it out and pressed the green button. "What?"

"It's me," Tobias said. "It's fucking too late, man. They're out to get you."

"Fuck! Fuck! Fuck!" I'd hoped I would have more time. I'd expected the wrath of The Firm for betraying them, but there were complications I hadn't anticipated when I'd decided to go rogue. I used to only worry about my sorry ass, but as of a few hours ago, Heath's and my grandparents' safety rested in my hands.

"Where are you?" Tobias asked.

"Maine."

"What part? I can be there in a couple of hours."

THIRTY: THE REAPER

"Can you meet me in Belfast? I'll text you the address. Get us a truck if you can."

"I'll be there," he said. "Archer?"

"Yeah?"

"Stay alive."

"That's the plan." I ended the call and met Heath's inquisitive gaze. "His name is Tobias and I trust him."

Trust.

A word I never thought I would say, but as I looked into Heath's eyes and listened to Tobias and Zero, I knew I could trust them. I had to. I couldn't do this alone.

"Good," he said, reaching for my hand. "We need to go, Archer."

"Let's do it," I said, just as loud voices and vrooming ATVs erupted in the peaceful woods.

***

"What are you gonna say to them?" Heath asked. We parked my bike a block from my grandparents' home, waiting for Tobias to arrive. He was rubbing his hands on my stomach. The gesture was soothing, momentarily easing the storm brewing inside me.

"I dunno." There wasn't a script for this kind of meeting. How could you tell the people you loved that you were alive after they'd mourned your death? It'd been a decade since they'd seen me, I hardly looked like that teenager anymore. "What if they don't believe me?" I asked, leaning back. It'd been the one question plaguing my mind since we'd arrived.

"We have to try," Heath said. He kissed the back of my neck, his lips traveling to my ear. "I don't know how they're gonna react. But if I was them, I would be so happy to see someone I'd missed every day of my life. To touch them again. To hold them again."

Heath's voice broke when he spoke. The despair beneath his words was undeniable. He once mentioned his family, and I wondered if his sadness was brought on by the memories of them. *We have to try*, he'd said. I'd never been part of a *we*, and as much as I hated to admit it, I found comfort in knowing that I had people I could lean on. I brought his hand to my mouth and kissed it, making a mental note to ask him about his parents and brother. "Will you come with me?" I asked.

"I'd love to," he said.

We jumped off the bike and walked to the house that used to be my home. It was a quiet evening. Everyone was probably asleep, dreaming, while I stood in my grandparents' doorway, hoping to wake them from their nightmare.

Heath squeezed my hand, nodding. "You can do this," he whispered.

I raised my shaking hand and knocked.

Thirty-One: The Priest

Half a dozen knocks later, each one louder than the last, light finally beamed within Archer's grandparents' house. There was the sound of shuffling feet, and the patio lights flickered on.

Archer placed his shaking hands in his pockets, taking deep and steady breaths. His emotions were all over the place, and I couldn't blame him. The stakes riding on this reunion were high, and coming face-to-face with loved ones who assumed you were dead would bring uncertainty even to the steeliest of hearts. As we stood, waiting for the door to open, I couldn't help but wonder about my brother, my only remaining family. He was alive. I believed that with every fiber of my being. Why else would he call me and send me a mysterious USB drive? I pushed those thoughts aside in order to stay present in this moment.

I kept a close eye on the road behind us, making sure The Firm hadn't made it to Belfast too soon, since Archer's mind was preoccupied. But aside from the handful of empty parked cars and his motorcycle, it appeared that we were safe. For now.

"Relax," I said, rubbing Archer's back.

He released a shaky breath when the door opened. An older woman answered, squinting.

"Who is it, love?" the voice of an older man asked from behind her.

Tears fell on Archer's cheeks and he didn't bother wiping them away. If you'd told me the man standing next to me, brought to tears by the sight of his grandparents, was a lethal assassin, I wouldn't have believed you. But that was one of the many beautiful contradictions about this man.

"Can we help you, gentlemen?" his grandma asked, reaching into a pocket of her robe, from where she pulled out glasses. She slipped the thick frames on, then studied my face first before her sight landed on Archer. She leaned closer to the screen door separating us and gasped, covering her mouth with her hand. Her body swayed, staggering back. If it wasn't for his grandfather standing behind her, she would've fallen.

"Easy, love," his grandfather said, steadying her. "Who do we have here?" He brought the glasses resting on top of his head to his nose.

His grandmother wasted no time and unlocked the screen door, rushing to Archer, who braced for her hug.

"Grandma," he choked, wrapping his strong arms around her petite frame.

"Oh my god." His grandpa joined us on the small porch, watching his wife and grandson. "My boy," he said between sobs. "Archer." He held Archer's face between his hands, wiping his tears away. "You're alive."

Archer attempted to free himself from his grandma's tight embrace, perhaps to look her in her eyes, but she shook her head repeatedly. It seemed like her hold on him tightened.

"No, no, no," she said. "I don't wanna wake up from this

dream."

"This is not a dream, Grandma. I'm here," Archer assured her.

Slowly, her wet face looked up into his. She pulled him down and peppered him with kisses. "How?" she cried.

His grandpa's hand combed Archer's hair before running his finger along the scar on his left eye. "My son. What happened to you?"

A red SUV with heavily tinted windows passed by. I followed its direction with my eyes, then turned back to the family reunion. "My name is Heath. I'm Archer's friend," I said. "Can we come in?" We needed to get off this porch.

Archer seemed to sober up from the tone of my voice, and ushered his grandparents in. "I'll tell you all about it inside," he said.

"I'll keep watch," I said, but Archer shook his head.

"Stay with me, please?"

I sighed. "Okay." I checked for the SUV before closing the door behind us.

Archer and his grandparents sat around the dining room table while I stood in the living room next to the window, where I could keep an eye outside. As much as I understood the importance of this meeting, we needed to keep it brief and get going if we wanted a fighting chance against The Firm. *A few more minutes*, I told myself.

His grandpa slammed the table with his fist, shaking his head. "They killed your parents?"

Archer reached for his hand, holding it, while his other hand rubbed his grandmother's arm, consoling her as she wept.

"How much more pain are they going to put you through? They have to pay for all of the things they've done," she said, hiccupping. She rubbed her chest, and my heart broke for the despair in her face. She'd known so much grief.

"They will pay, Gram. I will make sure they do. That's why I need you to come with me." Archer's eyes bounced between his grandparents. "I know what I'm asking is a lot, and I'm sure you have a lot of questions, but I need you to trust me, please."

A buzzing sound coming from Archer's pants interrupted the heartfelt moment. He pulled his phone from his pocket, glancing at the screen. He looked at me; he didn't need to say anything anymore. "It's Tobias."

I nodded and took his cell. "Hello?"

"Who's this?"

"This is Heath," I answered.

"Okay … where is The Reaper?" he asked hesitantly.

"Archer is with his grandparents right now," I said, walking closer to the window, peeking outside.

"He has grandparents? And who are you?"

"Long story, and I will have Archer answer them later, but are you here?"

"Yeah, red Tahoe a block from the address he gave me."

Well, that was a relief. "Great. I'll let Archer know. We'll be there soon." I hung up and joined the three of them, handing Archer his phone. "Tobias is here."

Archer looked at his grandparents' eyes, pleading.

"We'll go with you," his grandfather said.

"We don't want to ever lose you again," his grandmother added.

Archer exhaled his relief. He stood and rushed between them, wrapping his arms around their shoulders. "Thank you."

THIRTY-ONE: THE PRIEST

"Why don't you help them and I'll check in with Tobias?" I suggested.

"Okay," Archer answered, tapping my shoulder.

His grandmother grabbed his arm, as though a thought had just occurred to her. "All those flowers and presents over the years … were they from you?" she asked.

"Yes, Gram."

"Thank you. I kept them all."

I stepped outside and dialed Andrew's number. It kept ringing, but the phone connected before it went to voice mail. "Andrew?" Like the last time, nothing but static and beeping greeted me. "Where are you?" I whispered. It went unanswered. I ended the call.

A well-built man walked toward the house and I pulled the gun from my waistband, hiding it behind me. He was as tall as Archer and I, but more muscular than us both. He had short brown hair that matched his well-groomed facial hair. "Stay where you are," I said, pointing my gun at him when he entered the front yard.

He raised his hands, letting me know he wasn't armed, or at least not holding a weapon, since the outline of a gun was visible through his tight white T-shirt. "I'm Tobias," he said.

I lowered my gun and met him halfway. "Heath." I offered a hand.

Tobias shook my hand, his grip was strong and determined. "How do you know Archer?" he asked. "He's never mentioned you before."

"The Firm sent me to kill him," I confessed.

Tobias's eyes widened, and he pulled his gun out before I could blink. "What the fuck?" he asked, pointing it at me.

"Relax. I'm on your side." It was my turn to raise my hands.

"Where's The Reaper?"

"He's inside. He's alive," I answered. "His grandparents are coming with us."

Tobias glanced behind me, lowering his gun when he heard voices coming from the house. "Sorry, I don't trust a lot of people," he admitted.

"I get it. But I'm on your side."

"They sent you to kill him, huh?" Tobias tucked his gun back in his waistband.

"Yeah. They should've sent another Priest."

"Holy shit! You're one of The Priests?"

"Yup."

The door behind me opened. Archer carried two suitcases, while his grandparents carried one each. "Nice to see you alive, bro." Tobias grabbed the bag from Archer's grandma's hand.

"Thanks to him." Archer nodded his head my way. The tension in his face eased now that he was getting his grandparents to safety. We rushed to Tobias's car, making up precious time. The Firm could arrive any time now. "We need to go somewhere they can't track us," Archer said. He loaded all the bags in the back of the SUV.

I considered his question, a place coming to my mind. "I have one," I said. It was the hideout Andrew and I had bought years ago. We purchased it using a shell corporation we created overseas so it wouldn't be traced back to us. "Nobody knows about this place but me and my brother."

"Is your brother—"

"He's a Priest too." I didn't know how much I should reveal in the presence of Archer's grandparents, but it appeared that both Archer and Tobias understood what it meant. "We'll be

THIRTY-ONE: THE PRIEST

safe there. Trust me."

"Lead the way." Tobias pointed to the driver's seat before handing me the key.

I gave him the key back. "Actually, I'll ride with Archer and you can follow us."

Tobias raised an eyebrow, eyeing Archer, who shrugged. "You sure? You'll be more comfortable."

"I'm sure." When choosing between comfort or my arms wrapped around Archer, I'd pick him every time.

"Sounds like a plan," he said, smiling.

We helped the older couple into the jacked-up SUV. "Be safe, my love," his grandma said. She pulled Archer's face toward her and kissed his forehead.

"You take care," his grandpa echoed.

Archer and I walked to his motorcycle, his hands brushing against mine. "I got it," he said when I reached for the helmet. He put it over my head, his eyes never leaving mine when he fastened the snap. "Thank you, Heath," he whispered. "For everything." His gaze intensified, and I swallowed the lump forming in my chest.

Thirty-Two: The Reaper

We'd been on the run for hours and the adrenaline keeping me up was dwindling. A few more hours of this and I'd be running on fucking fumes. The purple sky signaled the dawn of a new day. A lot had changed in the past twenty-four hours, and with those changes came complexities in my simple plans. But I couldn't find it in me to regret any of my decisions.

We had crossed the state line into Vermont ten miles ago, and I wondered about our final destination. I didn't care where we went, but we were exposed while traveling and I couldn't stop worrying about my grandparents following us.

"How much longer?" I asked Heath, reaching back to caress his leg. I had no idea what the new day would bring, but somehow, having Heath fight this war with me was the extra push I needed to keep going.

"About thirty more miles," he said, tightening his arms around me. "Are you getting tired? We can switch." Heath rested his chin on my shoulder, rubbing our helmets together.

"Nah. I'm worried about being out in the open like this," I admitted. It was surprising how eager I was to tell Heath the truth. I used to say I wasn't afraid to die, but as I rode the stretch of black asphalt slicing through the forest with him, I longed for the prospect of the future. *Me. Thinking about the fucking future.* I had no clue what was budding between us. It was foreign to me, and it happened in the wrong place at the wrong time, but I hoped to live long enough to find out. I'd never been one to think about what-ifs. However, with Heath's arms wrapped around me, my hand resting on his leg, I wondered … what if our lives were different? What kind of future would we have with each other?

"Yeah, me too, but we're almost there," he said, easing my mind.

My cell buzzed in my pocket and beeped the incoming call notification through my helmet's speakers. Knowing that it could only be Tobias or Zero, I accepted it. "Tobias?" I asked, figuring I had a fifty–fifty chance of getting it right.

"This is Zero." Her voice didn't have its usual playful tone, which made me immediately tense.

"What's wrong?" I asked, holding my breath for the bad news. It had to be—that would teach me to think all mellow and soft.

"I just logged in to find where you guys are, since I haven't heard from you since you left the monastery—"

"Zero, get to the point," I urged. "Please."

"You're being followed. I can see twelve phones belonging to The Firm on the same road. Eleven in front of you are closing in and one behind you."

"Fuck!" I yelled. "How?"

"I have no idea. Nobody asked me anything, and even if they did, I would have sent them anywhere but where you are," Zero said, and I believed her.

"What's going on?" Heath asked.

"Someone's on our asses," I said, torn between slowing down and speeding up. They would catch up with us from either direction.

"Oh shit!" Heath said.

"Oh, and Reap …" She paused. "The solo dude driving behind you is El Jefe."

The mention of El Jefe's name made my world crumble. A rug was pulled from under me; one of the very few people I trusted and looked up to had betrayed me. I took a deep breath and asked, "How far away are they?"

"El Jefe is twenty-five miles away, and the guys in front of you are twenty. You have about twelve minutes to come up with a plan, man."

"Let me call Tobias. I'll call you later." I ended the call and called Tobias immediately.

"What's up," he greeted with a yawn. "Are we almost there?"

"We're stopping," I said, pulling the handbrake. Tobias's SUV behind us skidded to a stop. Heath and I jumped off my Harley and ran to the vehicle.

Tobias and my grandfather slid the windows open. "What's going on?" Tobias asked.

"Is everything okay?" Grandpa added, worry on his face.

Heath walked to the back-seat window and spoke to my grandparents. It was as if he could read my mind.

"We're being followed. Twenty miles that way"—I pointed to the road in front of us—"and El Jefe is twenty-five miles that way." I hooked my thumb over my shoulder.

"El Jefe?" Tobias asked in surprise. I didn't blame him, I was still catching up myself. "Are you sure?"

I nodded.

"Oh my goodness," Grandma said, wringing her hands. "Are

we in trouble?"

I walked to the back seat, opening the door. "Everything is gonna be all right." I held their hands to assure them. "But I'm gonna have you wait by the woods for someone."

"Why, son?" My grandfather asked.

Tobias opened the hatch and Heath grabbed my grandparents' bags.

I fought back tears and steadied my emotions. I needed to be strong for them. "We're being followed and we're going to keep driving because I don't want them to know you're with us," I explained. "And we need to hurry."

I breathed a sigh of relief when they moved to get out of the vehicle without any more questions. Heath and I assisted them. "We will be back," I promised. Heath and Tobias rolled their luggage behind some thick foliage, and we followed.

"Be careful, son," Grandpa said, hugging me.

"Come back to us, okay?" Grandma kissed my cheek. "All of you." She reached for Heath's and Tobias's hands, squeezing them. She returned her attention back to me. "We just got you back, we don't want to lose you again."

"I'll be back." It was an unfair promise, considering we had no idea which assassins we were up against, but I was out of words when it came to them.

"We'll be back," Heath and Tobias said in unison. Thank fuck I had them.

I dialed Zero's number and she answered after one ring. "What's the plan?"

"Can you find my exact location?" I asked.

"Yeah."

"Can you save it?"

"Yes, I can."

"Good. I have a huge favor to ask and I hope you'll consider it. I have my grandparents at this spot because I can't have them with us when we—"

"You want me to get them?" Zero interrupted.

"Yes—or send someone you trust. Listen, I don't know where you are, but—"

"I'll be there in forty-five minutes. I'll send a pic of me so you can show them." Thank fuck for Zero too. She knew we were short on time.

"Thank you so much."

"Hey, Reap?"

"Yeah?"

"Take care."

"I owe you one, Zero. And call me Archer."

"See you, Archer." She disconnected, and seconds later a text arrived with a picture of her.

"Grandma, Grandpa, this is Zero." I showed them her photo.

"She's beautiful, Archer," Grandma said, admiring Zero's rich brown skin and long black hair. "She's so young."

"She will pick you up in forty-five minutes. Don't do anything without her, please."

They both nodded before rushing to hug me.

"We have to keep going," Tobias said.

"Okay," I agreed, and the three of us ran to the road.

"Now what?" Heath asked as we reached the car.

"We fight." I opened my motorcycle's compartment and took an inventory of my weapons.

"What do you have over there?" I asked Tobias, pointing at the SUV.

"A lot," he said. "Rifles, pistols, grenades, knives, bulletproof vest."

THIRTY-TWO: THE REAPER

"Good." I handed Heath two pistols, which he tucked into his waistband. I did the same. "Let's drive seven or eight miles north of here. We'll make our stand far away from my grandparents."

They looked at each other and nodded.

"We have better chances if we make them come to us so we can control the surroundings," I explained.

"So, twelve versus the three of us? Not the kind of odds I like, but I'm ready," Tobias said.

"Four of us. The woods are on our side." I pointed to the trees lining the road for miles. Our only odds of having a fighting chance against a group of assassins was if we used the woods to our advantage.

"Let's go get 'em," Heath said.

We hopped on the bike and let Tobias follow us.

Eight miles north, we parked the bike and the SUV on the side of the road, making it easier for El Jefe and the gang to find us in our territory. Tobias handed us various weapons, loading us up with everything we could carry. We strapped knives to our ankles, and swung AK-47s over our shoulders, before filling our pockets with ammo.

"Are you ready?" I asked once we had everything.

"Bring 'em on," Tobias said.

"Ready," Heath concurred.

I leaned over and wrapped an arm around Tobias, tapping his back. "Let's stay alive, brother."

"Let's."

Heath pulled me in for a kiss and I cherished his lips on mine. "Don't die," he whispered, bringing our foreheads together.

"I'll try. You too, okay." I stole another kiss. Heath's eyes danced with emotion and I struggled to find the words I wanted to say to him.

"Tell me later," he said, sensing the battle in my heart.

"I will."

"Let's spread out," Tobias suggested, and we scattered, finding cover. *Stay alive*. That was the goal.

I leaned against the trunk of a giant pine tree, facing away from the road. I held the AK-47 close to my chest, waiting for the fuckers to show up. They would be here any moment, and we were ready for them. I couldn't fucking believe El Jefe pretended like he didn't know what was going on. So much for considering me a son.

I searched for Heath and found him about a hundred yards away from me. He peeked to his side, perhaps looking for me, and I gave him a thumbs-up when our eyes connected. Soft whistling coming from the trees above caught our attention. Heath pointed up to my left, where Tobias had camped on one of the thick branches.

Heavy tires crunched the ground and several cars rolled to a stop. I motioned to my eye then pointed to the road to let Heath and Tobias know they'd arrived. They nodded, turning toward the newcomers' direction, ready for combat. One by one, the doors opened and shut. They didn't even try to conceal their arrival. They clearly had underestimated us. The snapping of twigs and voices grew louder as they neared us.

Tobias pulled the pin of the grenade and threw it in the direction of The Firm's assassins. Heath and I covered our ears in time for the explosion. Screams followed the vibrations; the air was thick with dirt, leaves, and smoke, while shrapnel of branches and bark lodged within the perimeter of the explosion.

THIRTY-TWO: THE REAPER

I peeked to my side and fired the first shot, hitting one of the men trying to find his way through the debris in his chest. They fired back, but without knowing where their targets were, all they managed to shoot were the trees around us. They pushed forward and fired more shots, encroaching on our hiding places. I took a deep breath before pivoting to my left, firing my gun at a dirt-covered figure.

Something dropped feet away from where I had been hidden. It was followed by an explosion of dirt and smoke. I coughed as my mouth filled with hot dirt, spitting out the debris. It missed me by merely a foot. I blew out a breath when I realized how close I came to being blasted into pieces. "Fuck!" I turned around and fired back while Tobias and Heath covered my back until I made it to the next sequoia to find a safe harbor.

Tobias climbed down from his branch, pitching more explosives in their direction once he made it to the ground.

Heath and I exchanged shots with our enemies, but my vantage point was obscured by more trees in front of me. Some of the assassins found where Heath was hiding and blasted a barrage of gunshots, brown tree bark splintering in the air. He ran, dodging the bullets piercing every leaf and bush around him.

The three of us fled deep into the woods, glancing behind us intermittently to see how many of them were still standing. "Fuck," I said as a fallen branch caught my foot, tripping me. I propelled forward, facedown, my AK-47 hurling out of reach. Tobias and Heath stopped, but I urged them to keep running. Heath hesitated. "Run!" I yelled. He mouthed *Fuck,* but kept going.

I pulled the gun from my waistband and rolled onto my back as one of The Firm's assassins towered over me, kicking the gun out of my hand. He aimed his gun at my head.

A single bang reverberated. The hands of the man standing over me fell to his side. His gun dropped to the ground along with his lifeless body, a bullet hole in his forehead.

I scrambled up and looked behind me to find the source of the bullet. Shock couldn't even begin to describe how I felt as El Jefe rushed toward me.

"I got you, son," he said, extending a hand, pulling me up.

I picked up my gun and we ran, more bullets ricocheting around us.

"I don't understand," I said, shaking my head. "I thought you brought them here." We took shelter in a cluster of trees, El Jefe peeking to his side.

"I'd been trying to get a hold of you to warn you, but you left your phone in your apartment," he explained. "Archer, you should've come to me."

Speechless, I pulled him close and wrapped my arms around him.

"It's okay," El Jefe said.

"I thought you—"

"They will have to kill me first to get you, son," he said through gritted teeth. "Those sons of bitches will pay for their crimes."

"Did you know?" I asked.

"Just a couple of days ago. When they told me to assemble a team to hunt you down. A backup for someone who goes by the name The Bishop." El Jefe shook his head. "We'll make them pay."

The Bishop was Heath. There was no time to discuss him, so instead I asked, "How did they find me?" I thought we'd been careful, but I should've known better—this was The Firm, after all.

"They followed you from your grandparents' home," he answered. "Ready to fight with me?"

"Till the very end," I said, and meant every word.

Thirty-Three: The Priest

My legs grew heavier the further they took me into the woods, torn between running from our enemies and retreating to help Archer. Gunshots and footfalls and leaf rustling had overtaken the stillness of the forest; voices echoed through the canyon of trees while the bang of pistols popped like balloons. I glanced over my shoulder, wondering how many more were left standing. It was hard to tell; they appeared to have spread out like the three of us.

My attention went back to Archer. My heart lodged in my throat at the prospect of him being caught. "He's got this," I said, convincing myself. He was The Reaper, after all. I sprinted the last few yards between me and the car-sized boulder wrapped in green moss ahead, dodging the strings of bullets coming from behind me.

A piercing force hit my back, causing me to fall to the ground, the impact knocking the wind out of me. I'd been hit, and if it wasn't for the protection of my bulletproof vest, I would've been in a much dire condition.

I pulled myself up, taking deep breaths to calm the dull ache radiating below my shoulder blade. Once back on my feet, I

THIRTY-THREE: THE PRIEST

scurried to the boulder for cover.

I sat with my back against the giant rock. It vibrated as a barrage of shots ricocheted off it. Their gunfire ceased momentarily. It was the opening I desperately needed to shoot back. I peeked to my side, aiming my pistol at the man rushing toward me. After a dozen shots, my gun clicked—its clip had fired its last bullet. I released the empty magazine, reloading my ammunition with the one strapped to my waist. I resumed my position, my body shielded by the rock, my hand extended, directed at my enemy, but he reached me before I managed to fire.

He kicked my hand and the gun flew into the air, landing ten feet from us. I yanked his leg and he lost his balance, landing on his back. He turned to crawl to pick up his weapon, but I dragged him back by his feet, his hands grabbing dried leaves instead. He rotated his body, his back to the ground, and swung a leg, his boot connecting with my right cheek.

"Shit!" I touched the spot, which hurt like hell. We stood, and I jumped on his back when he beelined for his gun. Gravity pulled us back to the ground, and I swung my fist at his ear, pain discharging through my hand as my knuckles connected. He grunted in pain before he pushed off the ground and elbowed my side to get me off his back. We rolled, wrestling for control, until his back slammed into a thick trunk. Though he was momentarily stunned, we continued to exchange hit for hit.

I heard screaming and commotion between our grunts and heavy breathing, and was relieved when the faint sound of Tobias's and Archer's voices carried through the woods. I had the man pinned to the ground between my legs and he squirmed. He reached for a rock at his side and swung it toward my head, knocking me on my back.

We'd traded positions. My eyesight was blurry, and I felt disoriented from the blow. I scrabbled around for any solid object within reach and found nothing but moss-covered twigs. A figure appeared above me, and I shook my head repeatedly to focus my vision.

The man straddling me reached for the larger rock next to him. I punched his stomach, but, like me, he was wearing a bulletproof vest. He lifted both arms over his head, the rock aimed at my face. Three shots were fired behind him, and I was splattered with blood and other matter as a bullet sliced through his skull. He fell into my arms.

I pushed his dead body off and sat up, expecting to find either Archer or Tobias, but it was neither who saved me. I blinked my eyes in disbelief, hoping my mind wasn't playing tricks on me. "Andrew?"

He rushed toward me, extending his hand to help me stand. I hugged him and he wrapped his arms around me. "You're alive," I said.

"I am, but we have to go," he said as he released me. He looked different. His hair was longer and a beard hugged his face. If it wasn't for his blue eyes, the ones matching mine, I wouldn't have recognized him.

"How did you get here?" I asked.

"I've been watching you for months. I knew the Church and The Firm would go after you because of what I discovered." He looked around, wariness in his eyes.

"What did you find?"

"Gruesome things. Things they had all of us do." His hands gripped the sides of my face. "The people we killed ... most of them were innocent." Darkness flashed across his eyes, his

THIRTY-THREE: THE PRIEST

hands trembling with barely controlled rage.

"I called you all the time and you never answered. Were those phone calls from you?" I asked.

"I didn't want to risk your life, but I needed to hear your voice to make sure you were still alive. I'm sorry, but I thought that was the best thing I could do to keep you from harm. I'd been in the shadows watching over you while planning my next move. That's why I sent you the list. It's safer with you, in case they get me first. That's why I sent you the photos, to let you know I was there."

Confusion clouded my brain. "That was a list?"

He nodded. "Do you still have it?"

"Yes."

"Good. We need to go. This way." He pointed toward the road with his gun.

"Wait, I can't," I said, stopping him. I couldn't leave Archer and Tobias. "I can't leave without my team."

The lines on his forehead deepened. "We have to get out of here before backup arrives."

"We have to find them." I took off in the direction I'd last seen Archer, with Andrew having no choice but to follow behind.

Andrew grabbed my shirt and pulled me behind a tree, pointing at three armed men ahead, sweeping the forest with their rifles. Shots were fired from above them, hitting one in the head. The remaining two fired back and so did we.

"Fuck!" Tobias yelped, grabbing his wounded leg before falling to the ground.

"Tobias!" I rushed to get to him while Andrew covered me. "Are you okay?" I asked, examining his injured leg.

Tobias grimaced, gritting his teeth. "My fucking leg," he

muttered.

"Can you stand?"

"I can try." Tobias sat up, sweat dripping down his face. Andrew draped his arm on his shoulder.

"Who are you?" Tobias asked.

"This is my brother, Andrew," I said. "Andrew, this is Tobias. He's one of us."

"How did you get here?" Tobias asked.

"We'll get to that later. We need to find Archer," I said.

We slowed down. My worry grew watching Tobias hopping on one foot. I didn't know the extent of his injury, but his pants were already soaked with blood. I was hyper-aware of my surroundings, making sure no one sneaked up on us while we searched for Archer.

"HEATH!"

The sound of my name had never been sweeter. *Archer.* He was alive.

"Archer, over here!" I called back. He appeared from behind a group of trees to our left, running when he spotted us. Archer's mouth found mine, gripping my body with his arms for all I was worth. "I'm okay," I said when our lips parted. My eyes fell behind him and met a pair I didn't recognize.

I drew my gun, pointing it at the man.

"He's with me," Archer said.

"El Jefe?" Tobias said.

So, this was El Jefe. *What's he doing here?* I thought he was *after* Archer. After us. "Looks like you've seen better days," El Jefe said.

"He saved my life," Archer explained. "He came to fight with us. He's on our side."

"I think we got them all, but I suspect more are coming. This is The Firm, they always have backup," El Jefe said, looking around the woods littered with dead bodies.

Archer eyed Andrew and Tobias before returning his focus to me. He stood next to me, intertwining our fingers. Andrew raised an eyebrow, his gaze bouncing between us. "Andrew," he said, proffering his hand. "Heath's brother."

"Archer."

"You're The Reaper," Andrew said.

"Let's do the whole family reunion later," El Jefe urged, leading us at pace to our cars. "We gotta go before they get here."

Archer's phone rang before we made it out of the woods. "Talk to me, Zero." He paused for a few seconds. "Fuck!"

We stopped; all eyes were on him. He pinched the bridge of his nose, looking up at the sky. "How many?" he asked, nodding and cursing some more. "I will." Archer ended the call and brought his attention to us.

"How many?" I asked.

"Three cars. At least eight men, according to Zero's tracker."

"Goddamn it." Tobias ran his hand over his short hair.

"Zero's working with you?" El Jefe asked.

Archer nodded. "She knows about The Firm."

"Good. She's a great asset to have on your side." El Jefe tapped Archer's back.

"What now?" Andrew asked, still holding on to Tobias.

Archer grimaced. "We keep going until we can't."

Thirty-Four: The Reaper

The rugged fifty yards between us and the road, where our vehicles were parked, was the longest dash of my life. I released Heath's hand and hurried toward Andrew, draping Tobias's other arm over my shoulder and wrapping my arm around his waist so Andrew and I could carry him together. Faster. I didn't know how much time we had before The Firm's backup caught up with us. Time was a commodity we didn't have. My brain feverishly thought of ways we could get out of this mess alive. It was the fucking reason why I didn't involve myself with anyone in the past, but as I fought with these men who risked their lives to battle with me, I couldn't find it in me to regret any of my decisions.

"Just leave me here," Tobias said. His injured leg brushed a small mound on the ground. He shut his eyes, releasing rapid exhales through his mouth. "I'm slowing you all down."

"We're not leaving you," I said.

"It's not worth it. Go!"

"You're fucking worth it," I said. "So save your breath. Not gonna happen." My phone rang and dread took residence in the pit of my stomach. It could only be Zero with more bad news.

"Man, there are two more cars behind the other three heading your way," Zero said when I answered.

Just when we thought we could finally take a breather, more shit was coming. "Damn it!" I looked behind, relaying the information to the others. The road was within reach. Our vehicles came into view.

"We're almost there," El Jefe said. Heath left Tobias with Andrew and took the lead with El Jefe, armed with guns.

"Was that El Jefe?" Zero asked.

"Yes, he's with us." We reached the road. "What's their distance?"

Heath opened the back seat of Tobias's red SUV then assisted us in getting Tobias inside. "Extend your legs," Heath instructed.

"Based on my calculation, you have fifteen to eighteen minutes to get the hell out of there," Zero said into my ear.

I told the others. El Jefe nodded and jogged to one of the parked black vehicles on the side of the road. "Check if they left the keys in that one?" El Jefe pointed to the car behind Andrew.

"Yes, they're here," he said.

"What are you thinking?" I asked.

"We'll barricade these two SUVs to slow them down, while I take some of them out," he explained.

Heath and Andrew hopped in the car and did as El Jefe instructed. They parked the cars side by side, blocking the narrow two-lane road.

"What do you mean while you take them out?" I walked the short distance between us. I didn't like the sound of his plan.

El Jefe's face softened. He held my face between his rough palms.

I shook my head repeatedly. "No," I said. "We can get outta here. I'm not going to let you do this."

"Do what?" Heath asked when he reached us.

El Jefe looked into our eyes, solemnity heavy in his voice. "This is our only chance to get away. You two know that."

I turned my back to him. I understood what he was saying, but it didn't make what he was asking us any easier. "No," I whispered.

"Archer, look at me," he said. I didn't respond. "Son." Loose rocks shifted behind me as El Jefe and I stood face-to-face. "You must go and finish what you've started. This is the end of the battle for me."

"It doesn't have to be." Why couldn't one thing go our fucking way?

"I never thought my life would matter until now," he said. "We're running out of time."

I couldn't speak, choking on my emotions. How would my life look without him? He was the father I never had. I wrapped my arms around him, soaking his shoulder with my tears, hoping my hold on him relayed what my words failed to do.

I loved him. I would miss him.

"I do too," he said, sensing my unspoken sentiment. "Now, go on and make me proud." He tapped my shoulder and headed to Tobias. "Take care of yourself, and always have each other's backs."

"See you on the other side," Tobias said, wincing as he attempted to reach for El Jefe.

El Jefe held Tobias's leg and closed the door. He faced Heath, Andrew, and I. "Get those motherfuckers."

Andrew squeezed his shoulder before opening the hatch to

get in the third-row seat.

"Thank you." Heath shook El Jefe's hand.

El Jefe nodded. "Take good care of him."

"I will," he said, heading to the driver's side.

"Thank you for everything." I gave him one last hug and ran to the passenger's side before I dragged him with us. I hadn't closed the door completely when Heath peeled off the road, speeding from zero to ninety miles per hour in seconds.

Watching El Jefe from my sideview mirror, he became smaller and smaller until he was gone. *Till we meet again.*

We drove in silence as fields of green flashed by. I dialed Zero's number and pressed the speaker while it rang.

"El Jefe stayed, didn't he?" Zero asked.

"Yes." My heart felt like it was being shredded into pieces. "Are they behind us?"

"No one is following you. Every phone has become stationary on my screen."

"El Jefe?" I held my breath.

"His phone hasn't moved either," she said. "I'm sorry, man."

"How are my grandparents?"

"They're in great hands. They'll be okay."

"Thank you, Zero. I'll call you later."

Heath reached for my hand and placed it on his lap. "I'm sorry about El Jefe," he said. "He loved you very much, and there is no better way to show you but to risk his own life to save yours."

"He saved us all," Tobias said from the back. I glanced to check on his leg. A black leather belt was now wrapped around his thigh, acting as a tourniquet.

"How're you doing?" I asked.

"I'll live," Tobias answered.

"Where is that list, Heath?" Andrew asked from the back.

"My pocket." His attention never left the road.

My curiosity piqued. "What list?"

"The list of innocent people who fell victim under The Firm."

My eyes widened in disbelief. "You've had it this whole time?"

"I didn't know it until today," Heath said, glancing in the rear-view mirror to look at Andrew.

"I sent it to Heath because it was safer with him than me," Andrew said. "The Firm sent assassins to take me out after they found out I had a copy of the list."

"We'd been trying to get that list for months," Tobias added.

"Why do you need it?" Andrew asked.

"We are going to expose The Firm," I said. I shifted in my seat to face Andrew. "That's why your brother was sent to kill me. Because The Firm found out about my plan."

"Holy shit." Andrew whistled. "How?"

"Marilyn Ellis."

"The badass reporter?" Heath asked. He pulled a USB drive out of his pocket and handed it to me.

"Yes," Tobias said.

"This changes everything." I stared at the USB. Finally, the break we desperately needed.

"It has all of the names," Andrew said. "Including Senator Evans."

I dialed a set of numbers I'd memorized. "Marilyn, it's Archer. You're on speaker phone."

"Do you have the list?" she asked.

"Yeah."

"Good. We need to do this fast."

"What do you mean?" I looked around the car; everyone's

attention was on my phone.

"I think someone has been watching me. I've seen this same black car for the past two days. It's everywhere I go. The office, the store, my house."

"Fuck. Are you in your house right now?" I asked. I wouldn't lose another innocent life because of my plan if I could help it.

"Yes, and the car is across the street." Marilyn's voice was laced with concern.

"Can you see the plate?" I asked.

"Yes. Do you want it?"

"Tobias, call Zero."

Tobias complied and, seconds later, Zero's voice came through his cell speaker. "Can you run a plate for us?" Tobias asked.

"Hit me with it," Zero said.

"It's a Massachusetts plate. 897 RTA," Marilyn said.

"Gimme a minute." Everyone remained silent while we waited, the only sound was a faint clicking of Zero's keyboard through the phone. "I'm in," she said. "Oh shit."

"Talk to us, Zero," I said.

"How bad is it?" Marilyn chimed in.

"It belongs to Bayview Holdings."

"Fuck." I leaned back in my seat and rubbed my forehead. My pulse gushed in my ears. I saw red.

"What's Bayview Holdings?" Marilyn asked.

"One of The Firm's dummy corporations," Tobias answered. "Marilyn, this is Tobias. I will call my connection with the FBI and send him your way."

"Is he with The Firm?" she asked hesitantly. I couldn't blame her. The Firm was a whole different level of fucked-up beast.

"No, but he has been monitoring The Firm for years."

"Okay …" Marilyn said.

"He'll protect you. We'll send him to take you somewhere safe," Tobias assured her.

Marilyn didn't respond right away. We were asking her to risk her life for people she hardly knew. I would understand if she wanted nothing to do with this. "Only if you want," I said. "You can back out any time."

A long exhalation came down the line. "I'm all in."

"Thank you. Stay where you are," I said.

"Do not let anyone in, Marilyn," Tobias added.

"They're welcome to try. I have the shotgun my dad gave me."

"Good. Keep it close. Goodbye for now. I'll call back once we figure out our next move." I ended the call and looked out the window. We were no longer on the highway, instead nearing a modern two-story house tucked into the woods. The exterior was a mixture of polished concrete and rust-colored panels, and the perimeter was guarded by a metal fence made from iron rods.

Heath entered a code into a small box at the gate. "We're here," he said. "We'll be safe here."

For now.

***

"Hey." Heath peeked his head through the doorway before making his way in. I'd offered to take the bedroom in the basement so Tobias could take the room on the main floor. It would be easier for him to maneuver with his injury.

"Hey," I said. I'd been camped inside since we cleaned up Tobias's wound. "How is he?"

THIRTY-FOUR: THE REAPER

"He's sleeping. I gave him painkillers and antibiotics." The mattress shifted as he sat next to me, our backs against the headboard. I'd wanted to keep to myself and process the reality that El Jefe was gone, but now that Heath was sitting next to me, all I longed for was to be with him.

"How did you learn to do that?" I asked. Heath had removed the bullet lodged in Tobias's leg and stitched his wound closed like a pro.

"Part of my training," he said, staring at our legs brushing together.

"Priest or assassin training?"

"Both." He chuckled. He joined our hands together, resting them between our hips. "Perfect," he whispered.

My chest tightened with tenderness, my brain screamed *run* with his nearness. "I'm not perfect. Far from it," I said. "If I'm honest … I'm a monster." I looked away, fearing he could see through me and find nothing but gloom and destruction.

"Look at me, Archer," he said, tilting my chin toward his, urging me to meet his eyes. "You're not a monster."

"I am." The Firm had made me a monster, used me as a weapon to benefit their greed and hunger for power.

"If you're a monster, then so am I."

"I have nothing to offer you." I stared deep into his eyes and found the promise of a future I hadn't looked for. I never wanted it until then—and I'd never been more terrified. "I love you, Heath. I don't know when it happened, how it happened, but I do."

"I love you too, Archer."

I pulled him in for a kiss, attempting to let our passion speak a language unknown to us both.

Heath shifted and moved on top of me, keeping our lips

locked. He hummed when I gripped his waist and slid my hand to the globes of his ass. We explored each other's lips, but, unlike the other times we'd shared similar moments, it was tender. He moved his hands under my shirt and I cherished his touch. Our lips parted momentarily, long enough for Heath to pull the hem of my shirt over my head. His lips were back on mine before the garment hit the floor. His mouth traveled to my neck, his tongue glided to my chest, to my abs, to my obliques.

I held his hands, stopping him from pulling my sweatpants down—well, *his* sweatpants, since he'd let me borrow his clothes. "Come over here," I said.

Slowly, he crawled his way back to my face. I kissed him one more time before turning him on his back. Heath's body shivered when I nipped his neck on my way down to his collarbone, before peeling my body off his.

I went straight to his sweatpants, the ones that matched mine, and pulled them down to his knees, along with his underwear. A grin spread across my face when his thick cock greeted me. I nudged his legs apart and placed my hands on his hips, pulling him closer so I could take his dick into my mouth. I wanted to get him worked up again before I showed him how much I craved him.

"Hmmm …" he moaned. "That feels good, Archer."

I knew he was in heaven when I played with the head of his cock with my tongue. He thrust forward, skull-fucking me. I gagged when his cock hit the back of my throat, but I kept engulfing his length like a champ. I raised my hand to Heath's mouth. He licked and sucked my fingers until it was slick with his saliva. I used the same fingers to play with his asshole, before sinking my finger deeper into him, moving it around to prepare it for my cock.

I tugged my pants off with my free hand while Heath took his shirt off. I glanced at my swollen dick, dripping with excitement. I spit on his hole before sliding another finger inside him.

Heath gasped. "Take all of me, Archer. I'm yours," he whispered.

He didn't say anything else. I reached for my bag sitting next to the bed and pulled a condom and lube from within.

With a hooded gaze, Heath watched my every move, his parted lips pulling me closer to them like gravity. We melted into each other's mouths, my tongue memorizing his taste. I tore the condom wrapper and rolled it onto my cock, slathering it with a generous amount of lube.

"I need you inside me," Heath moaned.

I lined up my hard-as-a-rock dick with his opening and slid inside, slowing down until I passed the initial resistance.

Heath was breathing hard, his eyes locked with mine.

Once I broke past the tightness of him, I pushed further, deeper, focusing on his face. His eyes rolled into his head and he shuddered, taking every solid inch of me.

"That's so good," he whimpered, moving his head side to side with pleasure. "Harder."

I positioned the insides of my elbows to the back of his knees and lifted his ass off the bed. I hovered over him, his ass fully exposed to my powerful drives, and went as deep as I could. I held inside before pulling out and sliding back in. My pace quickened as his body convulsed under me.

"You're so tight," I said. "So fucking hot, Heath. I need this, you, forever."

I'd never spoken words of affection like this during sex, but my love for him had overwhelmed me and I found the act even more stimulating. "I could shoot any second," I said, breathing hard and staring down at my future. He was such a revelation and watching him drove me crazy. I didn't just want him, I needed him.

I grabbed Heath's cock and stroked it in sync with my thrusts. "Keep that up and I'll blow," he warned.

"Go for it," I groaned.

My load was on the cusp of exploding, so I gripped his cock tighter and jacked him while my dick buried into him. The image was too fucking much for me to hold off a second more.

"Fuck!" I yelled. My balls were ready to nut.

"I'm coming, Archer!" Heath covered his mouth to stifle his pleasure.

The vision of him coming all over his abs and the sound of my name pulled the orgasm out of me. "Heath, baby," I growled. My body tensed as I shot my load into him.

Heath was bucking under me, and he let loose a loud groan when his load shot between us, covering us both.

We lay still, connected as one while we caught our breath and melted into each other. I didn't care about the sweat, the lube, or the sticky mess of our releases. Nothing else mattered, not even out battered body.

"I love you, Heath. Please be mine."

"I love you too, Archer. I'll be forever yours."

Thirty-Five: The Priest

Three Days Later

You could eat the tension in the air with a spoon—and possibly choke on it. The exhaustion, pain, and anxiety were visible on everyone's faces. Marilyn paced under the lights in front of the camera that would broadcast The Firm's darkest and most hidden secrets. The vile truth about their existence. She shook her hands dangling at her side and stretched her neck to the left then to the right, murmuring to herself.

Her nervousness was justified. What was about to happen would put her life in great danger, if it wasn't already based on the stories she'd told us about the last couple of days. There was no turning back from here, not for her and most definitely not for us. We would live in the shadows until the last grip of The Firm's power was extinguished—and heaven knew how long that would take.

She took a deep breath before correcting her posture, adjusting the microphone clipped to the collar of her navy blue pantsuit. Her black hair was pulled into a tight ponytail, and her red lipstick burst from her cinnamon-colored skin.

She looked like a woman on a mission.

The flat-screen television next to her flickered before an image of the late Senator Evans popped up on the screen. More photos appeared, surrounding Senator Evans's picture until the sixty-inch screen was filled with the faces of those who'd fallen victim to The Firm—including the ones we had personally killed. Their faces haunted us. We couldn't bring them back to life, but we could risk our lives to stop The Firm by clipping their wings.

Archer walked in, his eyes sweeping the room. He spotted me in the corner and headed over. My stomach fluttered, like it always did when he was around. He was the architect of this plan and I had no doubt it would work. Our expectations were reasonable, and it started by exposing them. The Firm wasn't built in a day, and we understood that taking them down would be a slow and painful process.

He planted a kiss on my lips. "I love you," he said before standing next to me.

"I love you too," I replied. It was the third time we'd spoken those words to each other, but it didn't make what we felt less real. I lifted his shirt discreetly to check all the cuts and bruises he'd sustained.

He held my hand, kissing the back of it. "I'm okay," he said. "How's your back?"

"Better." I nodded. "Are you ready?"

"I hope this fucking works."

"It will," I assured him, linking our hands together. "Look around." I pointed at everyone inside the small, crowded room. "How could we fail when we're surrounded by all of them? These men and women are willing to risk their lives for this, and no matter what happens, we won't stop until The Firm is

THIRTY-FIVE: THE PRIEST

exposed."

Archer was thoughtful for a second, taking in the scene in front of him. "I hope it's all worth it," he said.

Tobias limped toward us. The swelling on his face had decreased. If God really existed, I'd like to believe that we were brought together for a reason, and the reason would be shown to the rest of the world in a few minutes.

"Yes!" Zero, who had revealed her real name was Amarilys, raised her fists in the air. "Stay there, Ms. Ellis," she said, removing her headset. She jogged the short distance between the desk she'd been camped at for hours trying to figure out a way to hack world news and cable outlets to broadcast Marilyn's exposé. Archer didn't trust stations, and we agreed with him. If the list we risked our lives to obtain was an indication of how corrupt The Firm truly was, they'd have moles in all industries, including news networks. "Are you ready to do this?" Zero asked Archer. Zero's free spirit and lively personality grounded us. She was the light to our shadows, the balance we needed.

"I've been waiting for this moment, but it is no longer just about me. I want to make sure you all are ready," Archer said.

"Your call," Tobias said. "You orchestrated this."

"We're all in this together. We wouldn't be here if it wasn't for all of you," Archer argued.

"Yes, but you got us here," I said.

He glanced at Marilyn, who was reading her notes. "Are we sure the FBI agent who's taking her to safety after this is clean?" Archer asked. The persona he showed the world was the opposite of who he was inside. It was a side of him he rarely let people see. I loved him, and he loved me. We might not say it all the time, but our actions spoke volumes. We were willing to die for each other, and if that wasn't love, I didn't know what love was.

"Yes," Tobias answered. "I trust this guy and you should too."

"What about my grandparents?" Archer asked Zero. They had been a constant worry for him, and he would be devastated if something happened to them because of him. Going back to Maine and exposing the truth about his faked death had been one of the hardest decisions he'd ever made. But it was the right decision, because The Firm had been planning to use them as bait to blackmail Archer into abandoning his plan altogether.

"Your grandparents are fine. They'll never be able to track them to my cabin. That's the beauty of working off the grid," Zero said. "Only El Jefe knew my location, and The Firm had no idea I existed."

Archer seemed visibly relieved. "Thank you. I wished El Jefe was here to see this." He rested his hands on Zero's shoulders, studying the room once more.

Losing El Jefe had been tough on Archer. He died for us and we couldn't allow his death to be in vain. I hoped he was watching us wherever he was.

"Marilyn," Archer called, bringing his attention to her. "Are you ready to do this? You can still back out, but we really hope you don't."

She tossed her notes to the desk, away from the camera frame. "Let's make those bastards pay."

Archer smiled. "Let's make them pay."

"Roger that," Zero said, rushing back to her desk. She put her headset on and faced Marilyn. "On three."

Marilyn gave her a thumbs-up.

"Three." Zero frantically typed on her laptop; lines and lines of green and white code appeared on her screen. "Two." She glanced in our direction and Archer nodded. "One ... and we're live."

On cue, a somber Marilyn spoke to the camera. "Wherever you're watching, I'd like you to stop what you're doing. What you're about to see is a product of power that has gone unchecked for a long time. Months ago, I met a man who went by the name The Reaper, an assassin working for an underground society of vigilantes claiming to right wrongs. But that's only half of the story." She paused for dramatic effect and to give the viewers time to absorb her words. "These are the innocent lives who fell victim to The Firm's power."

Marilyn brought her attention to the television screen showing hundreds of images, listing the names of the important ones. Finally, the photograph of Senator Evans froze on the screen.

"You all remember him. Senator Evans was a great man. He was the senator we all wanted. Kind, fair, trustworthy, honest. Apparently, too honest for The Firm. He was going to expose them, but he was ambushed and killed on his way to his hotel before he had a chance. He trusted the wrong people and he paid the ultimate price."

Marilyn stalled, holding back tears, overcome by the weight of her revelations. She took a deep breath before continuing.

"My life is in jeopardy, but that is the risk I'm willing to take in order to make them accountable for what they've done. The Firm has infiltrated international governments, religious sanctuaries, and corporations. You name it, they have influence in it. I want you to pay attention to what I'm about to say next," she said. Andrew zoomed the camera in on her determined face. "Go to the website www.thefirmwillpay.com. The list of their victims, video footage, email correspondence, audio recordings, and all the evidence about The Firm's operations are posted there. Do it now before they take it down. Because they will."

Marilyn's video ended and the room stayed silent. Everyone gathered around Archer, Tobias, and I.

"You all know that this is just the beginning, but I understand if you don't want any part of it," Archer said.

He looked at Zero first. "I'm all in," she said.

"I'll be the face you need," Marilyn said.

"There's no stopping us now," Tobias added.

"We won't stop until they get what they deserve," Andrew echoed their sentiment.

Archer brought his attention to me, reaching for my hand. "I love you. Always, even if you don't want any part of it," he said, his eyes pleading.

He didn't need to convince me. I planned to be with him for the rest of my life. We'd found beauty in chaos. "I'll be alongside you until the very end," I assured him.

He nodded repeatedly, before planting a kiss on my lips.

"You know this means war, right?" Tobias asked.

Archer looked around the room at the people he trusted and loved, determination on his face. "And we're just getting started."

The End

About the Author

LGBTQIA+ Seattlelite author who loves to write men who love men. His background in Medicine and Academics are evident in his books. When he's not working and writing, you'll find him playing tennis, surfing and skiing. He loves connecting with his readers as much as possible

Follow him on Instragram @author_garry_michael to learn more about his current projects.

Also by Garry Michael

Break Point
Tennis's golden boy Travis Montgomery is at the apex of his life and his young career after winning the US Open yet, his mind and heart is somewhere else. Somewhere deep inside the closet of his past and the secrets he hides even from those who are the closest to him. He is flashing back on another time, another dream, and another love when he is reminded of the only success that eludes him.

Fresh out of medical school, Dr. Ashton Kennedy moves back to Seattle to complete his medical training and start the new beginning he has wanted since Travis walked away six years ago. The task is proving to be harder than he anticipated, especially when Travis returns waving a white flag. What will happen when these two men meet again after six long years? Will Ashton get his questions answered or will Travis' ambition force him even deeper into the closet?

Heartfelt and sometimes comical, Break Point is a story about friendship, love, forgiveness and living an authentic life.

All the Cuts and Scars We Hide

Ex United States Marine, Wyatt Miller, was living a low-key life keeping those around him at arm's length. Fearing that the shadow that had been haunting him for four years would swallow everything and everyone he touched, he commits to living a solitary life. Until one night when a beautiful stranger came to his rescue during one of the darkest points in his life.

Caught between his guilt and his love for his family, architect Kai Lobo left Hawaii in search of a fresh start and a new place to call home. What he didn't expect was to meet a mysterious stranger that will change the course of his quest for a new beginning.

What will Wyatt do when the only man that can save him is the same person who will drive him over the edge?

What will Kai do when the only man who can free him is the same person that reminds him of a ghost from his past?

Will Wyatt and Kai be able to see past their differences and rely on what they have in common to alter their futures?

All The Cuts and Scars We Hide is a story about healing, redemption and love.

All the White Lies We Tell

After missing out on the chance to represent the United States in the last winter games, Isaac McAllister's focus was second to none. He spent the past few years away from his family training for this moment. He had a dream, a dream that only came every four years and he would do anything he could to make it happen. Even if it meant breaking hearts along the way. Olympic gold was the prize, love would just have to wait.

Canadian Foster Donovan Jr. had it all. Money, fame, and good looks. But what his peers truly envied was his natural talent on the slopes. Two-time world champion and defending Olympic gold medalist, Foster would do anything to defend his status as the best of his generation and join the ranks of the greatest alpine skiers. Even if it meant crushing the dreams of the only man he'd ever loved.

What would Foster and Isaac do when the price of their ambition became a heartache for the other?

A dream four years in the making. Two countries. Two men. One Olympic gold medal. All The White Lies We Tell is a story about rivals turned lovers vying for the same glory.

All the Battles We Surrender

Time. That was what Sawyer Montgomery thought he had until he realized that it was running out. Now, all he wanted to do was right a wrong from three years ago. He made a vow to spend what little time he had left with Hawkins, the only man he ever loved. He would try everything to penetrate Hawkins' armor before it was too late.

Time. That was what Jace Hawkins needed more of to forget his estranged husband. But after three long years, Sawyer showed up at the Alaskan home where they had promised to spend the rest of their lives together. The anger he thought he'd feel at seeing Sawyer again was nowhere to be found. Instead, it was replaced by an overwhelming fear of losing his lost love forever.

One man is battling to save his life, while the other fight to protect his still aching heart. To which battles are Sawyer and Hawkins willing to surrender?

All the Battles We Surrender is a story about second chances and valuing what everyone wishes for near the end.

Time.